GEORGE AT THE FORT

Or, Life Among the Soldiers

HARRY CASTLEMON

1st WORLD
LIBRARY
Literary Society

George at the Fort

Harry Castlemon

© 1st World Library, 2007
PO Box 2211
Fairfield, IA 52556
www.1stworldlibrary.com
First Edition

LCCN: 2007930793

Softcover ISBN: 978-1-4218-4835-8
Hardcover ISBN: 978-1-4218-4738-2
eBook ISBN: 978-1-4218-4932-4

Purchase *"George at the Fort"*
as a traditional bound book at:
www.1stWorldLibrary.com/purchase.asp?ISBN=978-1-4218-4835-8

1st World Library is a literary, educational organization
dedicated to:

- Creating a free internet library of downloadable ebooks

- Hosting writing competitions and offering book publishing
scholarships.

1ˢᵗ World Library Literary Society

Giving Back to the World

"If you want to work on the core problem, it's early school literacy."

- James Barksdale, former CEO of Netscape

"No skill is more crucial to the future of a child, or to a democratic and prosperous society, than literacy."

- Los Angeles Times

"Literacy... means far more than learning how to read and write... The aim is to transmit... knowledge and promote social participation."

- UNESCO

"Literacy is not a luxury, it is a right and a responsibility. If our world is to meet the challenges of the twenty-first century we must harness the energy and creativity of all our citizens."

- President Bill Clinton

"Parents should be encouraged to read to their children, and teachers should be equipped with all available techniques for teaching literacy, so the varying needs and capacities of individual kids can be taken into account."

- Hugh Mackay

CONTENTS

CHAPTER I

DISCONTENTED RECRUITS

"Captain, this thing must be stopped. I say it must be stopped, even if we have to resort to summary measures. We must find out who the ringleaders are, and make an example of them."

The speaker was Colonel Brown, the commanding officer of Fort Lamoine. As he uttered these emphatic words he slammed a paper-weight down upon a pile of reports which the adjutant had just brought in, and, settling back in his chair, looked sharply at the officer who stood in front of the table. The red sash the latter wore around his waist proclaimed him to be the officer of the day.

"How many did you say there were in the party who deserted last night?" continued the colonel.

"Seven, sir," replied the officer of the day, "and there is a list of their names. They took no horses with them, but they each secured a carbine and a box of cartridges."

"That makes thirty men who have deserted since I took command of this post," said the colonel, angrily, "and not more than half of them have been captured.—Orderly, tell

Corporal Owens I want to see him. He is one of the few non-commissioned officers in the command whom I am not afraid to trust.—Captain, have six picked men, with two days' rations, detailed to go with him in pursuit of these deserters. He can find and arrest them if anybody can."

The officer of the day closed the door of the colonel's head-quarters behind him, and in a few minutes the orderly opened it again to admit a sturdy young soldier, about eighteen years old, who wore upon his arms the yellow *chevrons* of a corporal of cavalry. This was Bob Owens—the boy who stole the *mail-carrier's* hard-earned money and ran away from home to enjoy it. He had not changed much in appearance. He had grown taller and his shoulders were broader, but any one who had known him before he entered the army would have recognized him now. The fact that he had been selected to perform the hazardous duty of pursuing and arresting the deserters who had left the fort the night before fully armed, and who would not hesitate to make a desperate resistance rather than allow themselves to be taken back to stand the punishment that would be inflicted upon them by a court-martial, and the colonel's declaration that he was one of the few non-commissioned officers in the command whom he was not afraid to trust, seemed to indicate that our old friend Bob had won a reputation since he enlisted in Galveston, nearly a year ago, and done something to win the confidence of his superiors. Let us go back and see what it was.

The last time we saw Bob Owens he was just coming out of a recruiting-office, having enlisted in the regular cavalry and sworn away his liberty for a long term of years. He did not take this step of his own free will, but was driven to it by force of circumstances.

When Bob found Dan Evans in his camp in the woods and

Harry Castlemon

stole from him the money that David, with Dan and Bert Gordon's assistance, had earned by trapping quails, he ran away from home, and after escaping from the constable who arrested him at Linwood on suspicion of being a horse-thief he took passage on board the steamer Sam Kendall for St. Louis. While he was on the steamer he made the acquaintance of George Ackerman, who was one of the pilots, and whom he twice saved from drowning. George owned an extensive cattle-ranche in Texas, which was held in trust for him by his uncle, John Ackerman, who was his guardian. After the Sam Kendall was burned he tried to show his gratitude to his preserver, whom he believed to be alone in the world, by offering him a home at his house. At first Bob was inclined to refuse. His imagination having been excited by the cheap novels he had read, he had left home intending to go on the Plains and make himself famous as a hunter and Indian-fighter; but George, who had seen more than one professional hunter in his frontier home, said so much against it, and painted the poverty and worthlessness of this class of men, and the dangers of the life they led, in such gloomy colors, that Bob was finally induced to give up his long-cherished idea, and to consent to accompany his new friend to his home in Texas. As George had no money, Bob footed all their bills, and in due time, in spite of the efforts which Uncle John Ackerman made to separate them in New Orleans, they arrived in Galveston.

They had scarcely stepped ashore before their troubles began in earnest. Bob's pocket was picked while he was passing through the crowd on the wharf, and the boys found themselves alone in a strange city, without money enough in their possession to pay for supper or lodging, and no friend to whom they could go for assistance. They spent the night on the streets, keeping constantly in motion to avoid attracting the attention of the police, and when morning came they found a good-natured grocer who gave them a breakfast of crackers and cheese, and provided George with the means of writing to Mr Gilbert for money to pay his fare and Bob's by rail and stage-coach to Palos. If they could only reach that place, their troubles would be over, for George was well known there, and everybody would be ready to lend him and his new friend a helping hand. But Mr. Gilbert lived a long way from Galveston, the mail facilities between Palos and his rancho were none of the best, and the boys were utterly at a loss to determine how they were going to exist during the two or three weeks that must elapse before George could receive an answer to his letter.

The two friends passed the day in roaming about the city looking for work, but nobody needed them. When the afternoon began drawing to a close they were almost tired out, and George talked of going to some station-house to spend the night—a project to which Bob could not bear to listen. The idea of having a policeman's key turned upon him was dreadful; the bare thought of it was enough to make him gasp for breath. As he walked along the streets he was continually searching his pockets in the faint hope of finding the missing money tucked away in some unexplored corner, and finally he discovered fifty cents in currency in the watch-pocket of his trousers. His heart bounded at the sight of it. It was enough to provide him with supper and a night's lodging, but was not enough to pay for the same comforts for George.

When Bob found this stray piece of currency he was not long in making up his mind how to act. He resolved to slip away from George, and accomplished his purpose by gradually slackening his pace and allowing the young pilot to get some distance in advance of him, and then he turned down a cross-street and took to his heels. He made his way to a cheap lodging-house, ate a hearty supper and went to bed, wondering how George was getting on and where he would pass the night. The latter, as we know, fared much better

Harry Castlemon

than Bob did, and the latter made a great mistake in deserting him. His companion had not been gone more than a half an hour before George encountered Mr. Gilbert, the friend to whom he had written that morning, and who had come to Galveston on business. The two looked everywhere for Bob, but were finally obliged to abandon the search. The missing boy had disappeared as completely as though the earth had opened and swallowed him up.

The first question that forced itself upon the mind of Bob Owens when he awoke the next morning was, "What shall I do next?" A careful examination of all his pockets showed him that there were no more fifty-cent pieces in them, and he was obliged to confess to himself that the future looked exceedingly dark. He walked the streets in a very disconsolate frame of mind, and had almost decided that he would step into the nearest grocery-store and ask the proprietor if he would not give him a job of sawing wood to pay for something to eat, when he happened to pass a recruiting-office. A sign posted up in front of the door conveyed to the public the information that men were wanted there for the United States cavalry service, and suggested an idea to Bob. He took a few minutes in which to run it over in his mind, and then faced about and entered the office.

The law against enlisting minors without the consent of their parents or guardians is very strict, but Bob got around it by repeating the story he had told George Ackerman, that he was an orphan, and that there was no one who had a right to control his actions. The recruiting-officer was a young man, not more than two or three years older than himself, but he had seen service away up in the Yellowstone country, and the scar on his forehead, which was not yet fully healed, marked the track of the Indian bullet which had come very near putting an end to his career as a soldier. Being unable to do duty in the field, he had been sent to Texas to recuperate his health and to recruit men to fill up some of the depleted cavalry regiments. He questioned Bob very closely, but the latter gave satisfactory replies, and, having passed the surgeon, his "descriptive list" was taken and he was duly sworn into the service. There were a number of newly-enlisted men hanging about the office waiting to be ordered to some post, and one of them, who acted as quartermaster-sergeant, took Bob into a back room and served out a uniform to him.

"What shall I do with my citizen's rig?" asked Bob as he twisted himself first on one side and then on the other to see how he looked in his new clothes. "I suppose I can't keep it?"

"Of course not," was the sergeant's quick reply. "It would come too handy in case you should make up your mind to desert."

"I shall never make up my mind to any such thing," exclaimed Bob, indignantly. "I have gone into this business with my eyes open, and I am going to see it through."

"That's the right spirit," said the sergeant. "But wait till you have ridden twelve hundred miles at a stretch in pursuit of a band of hostiles, and perhaps you'll weaken."

"What do you know about hostiles?" asked Bob.

"Well, I should think I ought to know all about them, for I have been there. This is my third enlistment in the regular army."

"Is that so?" exclaimed Bob. "I should think that after so many years' service you ought to be an officer."

"I was a non-com when I was discharged, and that is as high

as any enlisted man can get now," replied the soldier. "I was a captain during the war, but they don't take men out of the ranks and make officers of them any more. When I enlisted this time I had to go in as a private; but I have my old warrants in my pocket, and perhaps they will help me get a new one when I reach the post where I am to serve."

"What's a non-com?" asked Bob.

"Why, a non-commissioned officer," answered the soldier, staring at Bob as if he were surprised at his ignorance. "You never did any soldiering, I'll bet."

"No, I never did," replied the recruit; "this is my first experience."

"And before you get through with it you will wish that you had never had any experience at all."

"Don't you think I shall like the army?"

"Well, I know *I* don't like it."

"Then why did you enlist again?"

"Because I couldn't do anything else. A man who has soldiered for nearly fourteen years isn't fit for civil life. Now, make your citizen's clothes into a bundle and take them around the corner to a little Jew store you will find there. Mose buys all the recruits' cast-off clothing. He'll not give you much for them, but the little he will give you will keep you in gingerbread as long as you stay in the city."

"How long do you suppose that will be?"

"I am sure I don't know, but if recruits keep coming in as

rapidly as they have during the last few days, the lieutenant will probably take a squad off next week."

"Where will he take it?"

"That's a conundrum. A private never knows where he is going until he gets there."

"Where do you eat and sleep?"

"We take our meals at the restaurant next door, and having no bunks we sleep on the benches in the office. You can go about the city as much as you please, but you must be sure and report at meal-time. If you fail to do that, you will have the police after you."

"Why will I?" asked Bob in surprise.

"Because the lieutenant will think you have deserted."

Bob was beginning to feel the tight rein of military discipline already. At home he had always been accustomed to go and come when he pleased, and he did not like the idea of having his liberty restricted or of being obliged to obey without question the orders of a boy scarcely older than himself. But it was too late to think of that now. The youthful officer was backed up by the entire military and police force of the United States, and there was no such thing as getting out of reach of his authority.

"I am in for it," thought Bob as he rolled up his clothes and started for the little Jew store around the corner, "but I don't know that I could have done anything else. I shall have plenty to eat and a place to sleep, and at the same time I shall be earning money to pay off that debt I owe Dave Evans. What an idiot I was to keep that money! To pay for that one act of folly and dishonesty I am compelled to waste some of the best years of my life in the army. I hope I shall get a chance to show them that I am no coward, if I am a greenhorn."

It was little indeed that Mose gave Bob for the articles he had to offer for sale—just four dollars for clothing that had cost over thirty; but those four dollars made him feel a little more independent. They brought him a few delicacies to supplement the plain fare that was served up to him and his companions at the cheap restaurant at which they took their meals, and were the means of gaining him the friendship of one of the recruits, Bristow by name, who stuck to him like a leech until the last cent had been expended.

Bob remained in Galveston nearly two weeks, and during that time he saw everything of interest there was to be seen in the city. Then he began to grow tired of having nothing to do, and took to hanging about the office as the others did, and making comments upon those who presented themselves for enlistment. He was glad indeed when the lieutenant mustered all the recruits one night and ordered them to report at the office the next morning at nine o'clock, sharp; but he was provoked because the officer did not tell them where they were going. This, however, only proved the truth of the old sergeant's words—that a private never knew where he was going until he got there. Bob knew that they were bound for Brownsville when a steamer landed them there a few hours later, and he found out that they were going from there to Fort Lamoine when they arrived at that post after a weary tramp of more than three hundred miles.

The recruits camped beside the trail at night, and during the daytime plodded along behind the army-wagon which contained their tents, blankets, rations and cooking-utensils. It was very fatiguing to all of them, and it was not long before Bob began to learn something of the dispositions of the men with whom he was to be intimately associated during his term of enlistment. The majority of them grumbled lustily, and even talking of deserting, and there were not more than two or three besides himself who bore the discomforts of the march with anything like patience. There was not much restriction placed upon their actions, and, although they were not permitted to stray away from the line of march during the daytime, they were allowed to visit any ranches or farm-houses that might be in the neighborhood of their camping-grounds. The people they met along the route were very liberal with the products of their gardens and with their milk, butter and eggs, and the recruits fared sumptuously every day; but it would have been much better for some of them if they had remained in camp at night and left the settlers entirely alone. Not a few of the men with whom they exchanged civilities unconsciously sowed among them seeds of discontent that were destined eventually to bear a fruitful crop of trouble. By endeavoring to live up to the sentiments they heard expressed on every hand, more than one of the recruits found themselves landed in the military prison at Fort Leavenworth.

"I don't see why you chaps swear away your liberty, and work for thirteen dollars a month, when you might just as well get forty and be free men," said a rancheman one night, after he has given Bob and three companions, one of whom was Bristow, all the milk he had to spare. "You'll soon get enough of soldiering, *I* tell you. I know, for I have tried it. It is a heap easier to ride around on your horse and watch your cattle while they are fattening themselves for market on the rich grass."

"But we don't happen to have any cattle to watch," said Bob.

"Who would give us forty dollars a month?" demanded Bristow, who was one of the loudest and most persistent grumblers among the recruits.

"You could get it almost anywhere in this country," replied the rancheman. "I'd give it to you, for one, and I know of a dozen others who stand ready to snap up the first man that comes along, no odds whether he ever herded cattle or not. You have made precious fools of yourselves, and you'll get a fool's reward. You'll have mean grub, hard work and poor pay, and be niggers to every little snipe who wears a shoulder-strap."

"We've found that out already—haven't we, boys?" said Bristow, as he and his companions reluctantly took leave of the hospitable rancheman and retraced their steps toward the camp. "We *are* precious fools to work for thirteen dollars, when we might just as well earn three times that amount, and be our own masters besides. There is no need that anybody should tell us that our officers will treat us like niggers, for we have found that out too. Look at that lieutenant! He rides in the wagon every day, while we have to hoof it."

"But you must remember that he is not strong," said Bob. "He has not yet fully recovered from the effects of his wound."

"I don't believe a word of it," declared Bristow. "He's just as able to march and cook his own grub and pitch his own tent as we are. It makes me sick to see how that man Haskins waits on him." (Haskins was the one who had served out clothing to the recruits in Galveston.) "But a blind man could see what he is working for," added Bristow. "He wants to get into the good graces of the lieutenant, hoping that he will be recommended for a non-com's position when we reach the fort. I tell you I have seen enough of soldiering already, and the very first chance I get I am going to skip out."

"I'll go with you," said one of the recruits.

"All right! Shake on that."

"You may depend upon me," said the recruit as he grasped Bristow's proffered hand. "Do you remember that big-whiskered, loud-voiced rancheman who gave us the potatoes the other night? He is sadly in need of help, and he told me that if I would come to his house, bringing three or four friends with me, he would give us citizens' clothes and hide us until the officers gave up looking for us. All he asked was, that we should agree to work for him for twelve months, and promise not to leave without giving him due notice."

"I am in for that," exclaimed the recruit who had not spoken before.—"What do you say, Owens?"

"I say I am *out* of it," was the quick reply. "If I did a thing like that, I never could look a white man in the face again. I have been guilty of a good many mean acts during my life—some that I would gladly recall if I could—but I am not mean enough to desert. Besides, I have no desire to have a bullet sent into me."

Bob's companions did not know whether to be surprised or angry at this plain speech. They stared hard at him for a moment, and then Bristow said,

"Are you really afraid of being shot? Well, I can set your fears on that score at rest. I know that the penalty for desertion in the face of the enemy is death, but we are not in the face of the enemy now. The country is at peace."

"I know it is nominally so," answered Bob, "but it is not so in reality, and never will be so long as these hostile Indians and lawless Mexicans continue to raid over the Texas border. If you skip out, as you threaten to do, you may rest assured that you will be brought back by force of arms, and if you resist you will be shot."

"How does it come that you know so much more than the rest of us?" demanded Bristow angrily. "You are not an old soldier."

"I am aware of that fact, but I have been talking to an old soldier, and that was Haskins. He told me that Major Elliot, one of General Custer's officers, pursued a party of deserters, and when they resisted he shot three of them; and Haskins himself was one of the squad that did the shooting."

"I don't believe a word of it," exclaimed Bristow.

"Neither do I," said another of the recruits. "Of course we expect to be pursued, but we shall take good care that we are not caught. Any of these ranchemen who want herdsmen will furnish us with citizens' clothing, and before our year is out the thing will blow over, and then we'll go home, and stay there."

"It won't blow over as easily as you think for," said Bob. "It will be known to your home authorities and to everybody else that you are deserters, and all the detectives in the United States will be on the lookout for you. If you want to live in constant fear of arrest, you can do it, but I won't."

Bob stuck to his resolution, and his discontented companions stuck to theirs. We shall see in due time which of the four made the wisest decision.

CHAPTER II

AN OLD FRIEND TURNS UP

The long, toilsome journey was completed at last, and late one afternoon the weary and footsore recruits found themselves drawn up in line on the parade-ground at Fort Lamoine. After the roll had been called and the colonel commanding the post had hurriedly inspected them, they were turned over to a sergeant, who marched them into the barracks. There they found about two hundred or more soldiers, who, as soon as the order was given to "break ranks," crowded about them inquiring for late papers and asking a thousand and one questions in regard to what was going on in the States.

Learning from the sergeant that no duty would be required of him that day, Bob spread his blankets in one of the empty bunks, and, stretching himself upon them, placed his hands under his head and looked about him with no little curiosity. Presently a young trooper, a boy about his own age, who looked as though he were just recovering from a long siege of sickness, approached, and, seating himself on the edge of Bob's bunk, began a conversation with him. Those of our readers who have met this boy before in citizen's dress might have seen something familiar about him, but still it is doubtful if they would have recognized in him—Well, we

Harry Castlemon

will let him reveal his identity. After a few commonplace remarks Bob inquired, as he nodded his head toward a soldier who was hobbling about the room with the aid of a crutch,

"What's the matter with that man?"

"Raiders," was the sententious reply.

"Been in a fight?" asked Bob.

The young soldier nodded his head.

"How long since?"

"Last full moon."

"I hope these fights don't occur very often."

"Well, they do—much oftener than I wish they did. I have been in two pretty hard ones, and that's enough for me. I suppose we shall have more of them now, for I understand that we have received orders to follow the raiders across the river and thrash them wherever they can be found."

"Were you wounded in one of those fights?" asked Bob. "Then you must be sick," he added when the boy shook his head.

"Yes, I am sick," was the reply—"homesick and sick at heart. I have been in the army nearly two years and a half, and I don't see how I can live to serve out the rest of my time. I am dying by inches."

"What did you come into the army for, anyhow?"

"Because I was a fool," answered the young soldier bitterly.

"Shake," exclaimed Bob, extending his hand; "I came in for the same reason."

"Did your parents give their consent?" asked his new acquaintance.

"No, they didn't. They live in Mississippi, and don't know anything about it."

Bob's long tramp had taken a good deal of spirit out of him, and somehow he could not muster up energy enough to tell any more falsehoods concerning himself.

"My parents live in Ohio," said the soldier.

"Then how in the world did you happen to stray down here to Texas?" asked Bob.

"I ran away from home."

"Shake," said Bob, again extending his hand; "that's just what I did."

The two runaways shook each other's hands in the most cordial manner, and instantly all reserve between them vanished. They were companions in misery and united by a bond of sympathy. The young soldier at once became very communicative. He had closely guarded his secret for more than two years, because there was not one among the rough men by whom he was surrounded who could understand or appreciate his feelings. But here was one who could sympathize with him, and it was a great relief to him to know that he could speak freely and run no risk of being laughed at for his weakness.

"My name is Gus Robbins," said he, moving up a little closer to Bob and speaking in a low, confidential tone. "I had as good a home as any boy need wish for, but I wasn't contented there; still, I don't believe that I ever should have left it as I did if circumstances had not smoothed the way for me. My father is the senior partner in the largest dry-goods store in Foxboro', and he had in his employ two persons, father and son, who are in a great measure responsible for all the trouble I have got into. The buy was a clerk like myself, and his father was our bookkeeper. They had a very wealthy relative, a rancheman, living here in Texas, and when that relative died it was found that he had willed his property to our bookkeeper, to be held in trust for his (the rancheman's) son. They came to Texas to take charge of the estate, and after a while I received a letter from Ned (that was the boy's name) inviting me to pay him a visit. As he sent me money enough to bear the expenses of the journey, I came; and I am very sorry for it. We got ourselves into trouble by shooting some cattle that had broken into Ned's wheat-field, and had to dig out for Brownsville at a gallop. Ned went squarely back on me, and as I had no money to pay my way home, and hadn't the cheek to ask my father for it, I did what I thought to be the next best thing—I enlisted. I am very sorry for that too, for there was where I made my mistake. I ought to have gone back into the country and hired out to some stock-raiser. Then I could have gone home as soon as I had earned and saved money enough to take me there; but now I must stay my time out; that is, unless—"

Gus paused and looked at Bob. The latter understood him. Here was another fellow who had made up his mind to desert at the first opportunity.

"Don't do that," said Bob, earnestly. "You'll only get yourself into trouble if you attempt it."

"I don't care if I am shot for it. I'll make a break for liberty the very first good chance I get."

The tone in which these words were uttered satisfied Bob that it would be of no use whatever to argue the matter. It was plain that Gus had made up his mind after mature deliberation, and that he was not to be easily turned from his purpose.

"Where did your friend Ned go after you reached Brownsville?" asked Bob, who was much interested in the young soldier's story.

"I don't know; I left him at the hotel. He will come to some bad end, and so will his father, for they are both rascals. The property of which they have charge, and which brings in a big fortune every year, rightfully belongs to George Ackerman, Ned's cousin; but Ned and his father—"

"George Ackerman?" exclaimed Bob, starting up in his bunk.

Gus nodded his head, and looked at the recruit in great surprise.

"Is he a cub pilot?" continued the latter.

"'A cub pilot'?" repeated Gus. "No, he's a herdsman, or I ought rather to say he *was* a herdsman. He had stock of his own worth six thousand dollars. Where he is now I don't know, for on the morning after we left his ranche, while we were camped in the edge of the timber making up for the sleep we had lost the night before, we were surprised by a couple of Greasers, who made a prisoner of George and carried him across the river into Mexico. I don't know what they did with him, for all George could induce them to say was that 'Fletcher wanted to see him.'"

"It's the same fellow," exclaimed Bob, rising from his blanket and seating himself on the edge of the bunk by his companion's side. "He told me all about it, but his story was so very remarkable that I didn't know whether to believe it or not. He gave those Greasers the slip, secured a berth as cub pilot on a Mississippi River steamer, and that was where I found him."

With this introduction Bob went on to tell how he had saved George from going to the bottom when Uncle John Ackerman pushed him overboard from the Sam Kendall; related all the thrilling incidents connected with the burning of the steamer; described how Uncle John had tried to separate them in New Orleans; in short, he gave a truthful account of his intercourse with the cub pilot up to the time he deserted him in Galveston. Bob was heartily ashamed of that now, and could not bear to speak of it.

"I became separated from him in some way—it is very easy to lose a companion in the crowded streets of a city, you know— and that was the last I saw of him," said Bob in conclusion; and when he told this he forgot that he had afterward seen George go into a hotel accompanied by Mr. Gilbert. "Then I didn't know what to do. I had no money; I was hungry and sleepy, utterly discouraged; and, like you, I sought to end my troubles by enlisting. I see now that I made a great mistake, but I am going to serve faithfully during my term of enlistment, if I live. Is George's ranche far from here?"

"I don't know, for I am not much acquainted with the country east of here, never having scouted in that direction. It is about one hundred and fifty miles from Palos, if you know where that is. As you are George's friend, I am sorry that you enlisted, for I know that you are going to have a hard time of it; but since you *did* enlist, I am glad you were ordered to this post, for misery loves company, you know. Let's walk out on the parade, where we can talk without danger of being overheard. Perhaps you would like to take a look at the place which will always be associated in your mind with the most unhappy days of your existence."

It was plain that Gus took a very gloomy view of things, and of course his discouraging remarks made an impression upon Bob, although they did not take away the interest he felt in his surroundings. Everything was new to him, and he asked a great many questions as he and Gus walked slowly around the parade toward the stables.

Fort Lamoine was situated on a high, rocky eminence which overlooked the surrounding country for half a dozen miles or more in every direction. The stockade, which enclosed about two acres of ground, was built of upright logs deeply sunk in the earth. The tops were sawed off level, and a heavy plate of timber, through which stout wooden pins had been driven into the end of each log, held them firmly in their place. The officers' quarters, barracks, store-houses and stables were built in the same manner. On the outside of the parade were long rows of stately cottonwood trees, interspersed with shrubs and flowers. In one corner, on the right-hand side of the principal gate, was the well that supplied the garrison with water, and in the other was the flagstaff, from which floated the Stars and Stripes.

"Emblem of liberty!" said Gus with a sneer as he pointed up at the flag—"emblem of tyranny, rather."

"What do you mean by that?" demanded Bob quickly.

"Oh, you will find out before you have been here long," replied Gus, shaking his head and looking very wise. "A bigger lot of tyrants than the officers who command us were never crowded into any one post."

Harry Castlemon

"Perhaps you don't do your duty as well as you might?" mildly suggested Bob.

"I know I don't. I do no more than I am obliged to do, I tell you, and for the simple reason that I didn't enlist to act as lackey to a lot of shoulder-straps. I am just as good as they are, but they say I am not. Why, the last time the paymaster was here his little snipe of a clerk remarked in my hearing that enlisted men were nothing more than servants to the officers. What do you think of that?"

Bob did not know what to think of it, so he said nothing in reply. He simply resolved that he would not pass judgment upon his superiors until he had had some experience with them himself.

"This is by no means the gloomy place that I expected to find it," said Bob as he and Gus resumed their walk.

"Oh, the fort itself is good enough," replied Gus; "it's the people who live in it that I object to. If one could pick his own company, and could do as he pleased, he might manage to live here for a few years very comfortably; but we have to associate with some rough characters there in the barracks, and the officers hold us with our noses close to the grindstone all the time. They look upon a private as little better than a dog, and they'll slap him into the guard-house on the slightest provocation. Now, this is one of the stables; it will accommodate seventy horses. Those you see in here are blooded animals, and they belong to the officers. The government horses are always picketed outside, except when there is danger of a visit from the raiders, and then they are brought in for safe-keeping. Now, take a good look at the stable, and then come out and take another look at the stockade. Every night there are two sentries placed over this stable—one at the front, and the other at the rear, between the stable and the stockade—and a guard sleeps inside. Would you believe that, after all these precautions, it would be possible for anybody to come into the fort and steal a horse?"

Bob said he would not.

"Well, it was done not more than two weeks ago," continued Gus. "One stormy night these two logs were removed from the stockade, and four of the best horses in the stable were run off. It must have taken hours to do the work, and although the sentries were changed while it was going on, no one knew that a theft had been committed until the next morning."

"Who did it?" inquired Bob.

"A couple of Comanches, who were surprised and killed by the squad that was sent in pursuit of them. The Comanches are acknowledged, even by the Indians themselves, to be the most expert horse-thieves on the Plains. Why, one night, when a scouting-party to which I was attached were in camp and fast asleep, a Comanche crept up and stole the lieutenant's horse; and in order to do it he had to cut the lariat that was tied to the officer's wrist. He got away with the horse, and never awoke one of us."

Gus Robbins had accumulated an almost inexhaustible fund of such anecdotes as these during his two and a half years of army-life, and he related a good many of them to Bob while they were walking about the fort examining the different objects of interest. From some of them Bob gained a faint idea of what might be in store for himself.

The next morning the newly-arrived recruits were formed into an awkward squad and turned over to the tender mercies of a grizzly old sergeant, who proved to be anything but an agreeable and patient instructor. He drilled them for four hours without allowing them a single moment's rest, abusing them roundly for every mistake they made; and when at last he marched them to their quarters, it was only that they might eat their dinner and take half an hour's breathing-spell preparatory to going through the same course of sprouts again in the afternoon. This routine was followed day after day until the members of the awkward squad were declared to be sufficiently drilled to warrant their appearance on dress-parade. After that they were assigned to the different troops (or companies) that stood the most in need of men, Bob, to his delight, finding himself in the same troop to which his new friend, Gus Robbins, belonged. But even then their troubles did not cease. Instead of drilling eight hours each day, they drilled six, and were obliged to do guard-duty besides. Among the three hundred and eighty men who composed the garrison there were not a few old soldiers who hated this hard work as cordially as some of the new-comers did, and there was a good deal of grumbling among them; but Bob Owens never uttered a word of complaint. Firmly adhering to the resolution he had made when he first enlisted, he set himself to work to learn just what was required of him, and when he found out what his duty was, he did it cheerfully and faithfully. He was always on hand when he was wanted, his equipments were always ready for inspection, and his horse shone like satin. When his own steed had been fed and groomed, he turned his attention to the horse belonging to the lieutenant who commanded the troop to which he belonged, and thereby aroused the indignation of some of his brother-soldiers.

"What are you doing that for?" demanded Gus Robbins one day as he and Bristow entered the stable and found Bob busy at work grooming the lieutenant's horse. "You are in pretty business, I must say!"

"Yes, I rather like it," answered Bob. "I always liked to work about horses, and I am doing this because I haven't anything else to do just now."

"Well, I wouldn't do it any more if I were in your place," continued Gus. "The law expressly prohibits an officer from compelling, or even hiring, an enlisted man to do his dirty work."

"It does, does it?" exclaimed Bob. "Didn't you tell me when I just came here that enlisted men were nothing but servants to their officers?"

"I didn't mean that, exactly," stammered Gus. "What I *did* mean was, that they don't treat us like human beings. If an officer wants a servant, he must hire a civilian and pay him out of his own pocket; that's what the law says."

"I am aware of that fact; but the law doesn't say that I shall not groom the lieutenant's horse if I choose to do it of my own free will, does it?"

"Let the toady alone, Robbins," said Bristow angrily. "The troop hasn't got all the non-coms that it is entitled to, and Owens is working for chevrons. You know the lieutenant said the other day that there were four corporals' and two duty sergeants' warrants waiting for those who were willing to win them; and this is the way Owens is going to work to get one of them."

Bob straightened up, looked sharply at Bristow for a moment, and then drew back the brush he held in his hand, as if he had half a mind to throw it at his head.

"That's what all the boys say, Bob," observed Gus. "If you want to keep on the right side of the privates, you must not try to curry favor with the officers."

"If you want a non-com's warrant, why don't you wait until you get a chance to win it in battle?" added Bristow. "That's what I intend to do, and I shall think much more of a promotion earned in that way than I should of one I had gained by cleaning an officer's horse."

"Look here, fellows," said Bob earnestly: "I don't do this work for the lieutenant because I hope to gain anything by it. I do it simply to pass away the time, for I can't see any fun in loafing about the quarters doing nothing. If the boys don't like it, let's see them help themselves."

"If the lieutenant was a decent man, I wouldn't say a word," answered Bristow. "But he is so mean that I wouldn't turn my hand over to save his life."

"Anybody with half an eye could see what is the matter with you," retorted Bob. "You have been in the guard-house about half the time since you have been here, and spent the other half in doing extra duty; and that's the reason you don't like the lieutenant. If you will wake up and attend to business, he will treat you well enough."

Bob's prompt and soldier-like way of performing the work that was required of him very soon attracted the attention of Lieutenant Earle (that was the name of the officer in command of the troop to which Bob belonged), and he took his own way to reward him for it. If he was ordered off on a scout, Bob Owens was always one of the "picked men" who accompanied him. If he was sent out with a squad during the full of the moon to watch the ford a few miles below the fort, Bob was one of the members of that squad. This did not excite the jealousy of the good soldiers, for they were always glad to have a brave comrade to back them up in times of danger, no matter whether he was a greenhorn or a veteran; but the grumblers and the discontented ones, especially those who belonged to his own troop, had a good deal to say about it, and declared that the lieutenant took Bob with him on his expeditions to pay him for grooming his horse. They disliked him cordially, and it was not long before an incident happened that caused the dislike of at least one of them to grow into positive hatred.

One pleasant afternoon some of the men received permission to go outside the gates for a short stroll. They wandered off in squads, some going one way and some another, and Bristow and two companions—one of whom was Gus Robbins—bent their steps toward the crumbling remains of an old adobe outpost which marked the spot where more than one desperate fight with the Apaches had taken place in the days gone by. There they seated themselves and entered into conversation, Bristow's first words indicating that they were about to discuss a subject that had before occupied their attention.

"I tell you, Robbins," said he, "if you are in earnest in what you say, now is the time to prove it."

"I certainly am in earnest," answered Gus; "but, to tell you the honest truth, I am afraid."

"'Afraid'!" repeated Bristow in a tone of contempt. "What in the world are you afraid of?"

"Of pursuit," replied Gus. "If we resist, we run the risk of being shot; and if we are captured, we stand an excellent chance of going to prison."

"Now, Robbins," said Bristow earnestly, "let me once more explain our arrangements to you, and you will see that we do not risk anything. In the first place, the horses are left picketed outside the stockade every night. They are never brought in, as you know, unless there is danger of a visit from the raiders. Four of the six men who are to act as horse-guards to-night belong to our party. When the time for action arrives, these four men will go to work on the other two and try to induce them to accompany us. If they don't succeed, they'll bind and gag them, and so put it out of their power to give the alarm. The sentry who will be on duty between the stable and the stockade is also one of us, and of course he will raise no objection when we slip out of the quarters, one by one, and climb the stockade. As fast as we get over we will select our horses—I've got mine picked out, and I could put my hand on him in the darkest of nights—and when the last one has made his escape we'll mount and put off. Of course we hope to escape by running, but if we can't do that, we shall turn at bay and make a fight of it. We have all sworn to stand by one another to the last, and thirty determined, well-armed men can make things lively for a while, I tell you."

Bristow continued to talk in this strain for half an hour, his companion now and then putting in a word to assist him; and he talked to such good purpose that Gus Robbins finally consented to make one of the large party that was to desert the post that very night. Bristow then gave him the names of the other members—there were several non-commissioned officers among them—and after urging him to be very careful of himself, and to say and do nothing that might arouse the suspicions of "outsiders," the three got upon their feet and walked toward the fort.

They had scarcely left the ruins when a fatigue-cap arose from behind a pile of rubbish scarcely a dozen feet from the place where the three conspirators had been sitting, and a pair of eyes looking out from under the peak of that cap watched them as they moved away.

CHAPTER III

BOB'S FIRST COMMAND

The eyes that were so closely watching the movements of Bristow and his companions belonged to Bob Owens. The latter had strolled off alone, and thrown himself behind an angle of the ruined wall to indulge in a few moments' quiet meditation, and thus unwillingly placed himself in a position to overhear the details of the plot which we have just disclosed. If Bristow had not so promptly entered upon the discussion of the subject of desertion, Bob would have made his presence known to him; but after he had listened to the first words that fell from his lips he thought it best to remain quietly in his place of concealment, for he knew that if he revealed himself, then he would be accused of playing the part of eavesdropper.

"Now, here's a go!" thought Bob, rising to his feet when he saw Bristow and his two friends walk through the gate into the fort, "and I wish somebody would be kind enough to tell me what I ought to do about it. Shall I stand quietly by and let them go, or shall I tell the officers what I have heard? If I let them go, they will run the risk of being gobbled up by that party of Kiowas who are now raiding the country north of us; and if I tell the colonel, and it should ever be found out on me, I should lead a hard life in the quarters. I wish I had

Harry Castlemon

been somewhere else when they came here."

Thrusting his hands deep into his pockets, Bob left the ruins, and, walking slowly around the stockade, entered at a gate on the opposite side. His first care was to hunt up the sergeant-major of his regiment, whom he found in the quarters. This man had grown gray in the service, and he was a soldier all over—brave, faithful and untiring in the performance of his duty. He readily responded to Bob's significant wink, and followed him out on the parade.

"Sergeant," said Bob as soon as they were beyond earshot of everybody, "I have accidentally come into the possession of a secret, and I don't know what to do with it. There are thirty men in the garrison who are going to desert to-night."

The old fellow took a fresh chew of tobacco, pushed his cap on the back of his head and looked at Bob, who, after telling him where he had been and how he happened to overhear the plot, continued:

"It would never do to let them go. You know I was detailed to act as the colonel's orderly this morning, and I heard that scout who came in just before noon tell him that there is a large party of hostiles between here and Fort Tyler. These deserters intend to take their weapons with them, and think they can make a good fight; but those Kiowas are strong enough to annihilate them."

"Small loss that would be to us!" growled the veteran. "We are going to have some hot work to do before long, and such men are no good in a fight."

"It would never do to let them go," repeated Bob, "but there is only one way to prevent it that I can see; and that is by telling the colonel all about it. If I do that, and they should find it out, they would go back on me, sure."

"Of course they would," said the sergeant.

"Well, what would you do if you were in my place?" asked Bob.

"What would I do? I would go straight to the officer of the day and tell him the whole thing. The good-will of such men don't amount to anything, any way, and what do you care if they do go back on you? There's only thirty of them, and that leaves three hundred and fifty good fellows who will always be ready to befriend you. Do you know who these deserters are? I'll report the matter if you are afraid, and then let's see one of them open his head to me."

Bob repeated the names of the would-be deserters which Bristow had given as nearly as he could recall them, and the sergeant hurried off to hunt up the officer of the day, while Bob went back into the quarters. He had been there but a few minutes when the orderly appeared at the door and sung out,

"Owens, the colonel wants to see you."

"Aha!" exclaimed Bristow, "our good little boy has been doing something bad at last.—There are no bunks in the guard-house, Owens."

Bob made no reply. He followed the orderly across the parade and into the colonel's head-quarters, where he found the officer of the day, the sergeant-major and all the ranking officers of the garrison. The colonel questioned him closely in regard to the plot he had discovered, and finally dismissed him and the sergeant without making any comments. Half an hour later the entire cavalry force of the garrison was drawn up in line, the names of forty men who were ordered to the

Harry Castlemon

front and centre were read off, and the rest of the troopers were sent back to their quarters. Then the bugle sounded "Boots and saddles!" and in a few minutes more these forty men—one of whom was Bob Owens—rode out of the gate, led by the scout who had brought the information concerning that war-party of Kiowas. The squad was commanded by Lieutenant Earle.

"That's all right," whispered Bristow to one of his fellow-conspirators as they stood in front of their quarters and saw their comrades ride away. "There will be just so many men less to follow us to-morrow morning. But I wish we knew which way they are going," he added in a tone of anxiety; "and we must find out if we can. We don't want to run into them if we can possibly avoid them, for there are some of the best men in the garrison in that party."

"I suppose we are off after the hostiles," said the soldier who rode by Bob's side. "The scout told the colonel that there were three hundred braves in that party, didn't he?"

Bob answered that that was what he understood him to say.

"Then I wish we had a hundred men instead of forty," continued the trooper. "Our squad is too large to conceal itself, and too small to make a successful fight against such overwhelming odds. Well, if worst comes to worst—"

The speaker thrust his hand into his boot-leg and drew out a loaded Derringer. He intended to send its contents through his own head rather than fall alive into the hands of the hostiles. Probably nine out of ten men in that squad were provided with weapons just like it, and which they intended to use in the same way should circumstances require it. Veteran Indian-fighters never fail to give this advice to a recruit: "When it comes to a fight, save the last shot for yourself."

But, as it happened, Bob and his companions were not out after hostiles on this particular afternoon, for that raiding-party of Kiowas was already beyond the reach of any force that the commander of Fort Lamoine could have sent in pursuit of it. They found out in due time that their mission was of an entirely different character. They rode at a sharp trot until it was nearly dark, and then they went into camp in a belt of post-oaks and cooked and ate their supper. After an hour's rest they mounted and rode back toward the fort again. Arriving within a mile of the stockade, a halt was ordered, the men were dismounted, and, every fourth trooper being left to hold the horses, the others marched off through the darkness, armed only with their revolvers. Then Bob began to understand the matter. The object of the expedition was to capture the deserters. It had been led away from the fort simply as a "blind," and in order to lull the malcontents into a feeling of security no change whatever had been made in the guards who were to do duty that night.

After the lieutenant had marched about half a mile another halt was ordered, and sixteen men, divided into squads of four men each, were told off to begin the work. The officer approached each squad in turn, and after designating some one to take charge of it, gave him his instructions in a whisper. When he walked up to Bob he asked,

"Do you know where post No. 4 is? and can you go straight to it without making any mistake?"

"Yes, sir, to both your questions," was the prompt reply.

"Very well. Take command of this squad and go and arrest Dodd, whom you will find on guard there. Then put Carey in his place, and come back and report to me at post No. 1, and I will tell you what else to do. The countersign," added the lieutenant, coming a step nearer to Bob and speaking in a tone so low that no one else could catch his words, "is 'Custer.' Be quick and still. Forward, march!"

As Bob moved away with his squad he told himself that fidelity is sometimes appreciated. This was his first command, and he knew that much depended upon the way in which he executed the orders that had been given him. If they were faithfully and skilfully carried out, he might hope to be entrusted with other commands in future, and so be given opportunities to distinguish himself and win promotion; for Bob, like every ambitious boy, was anxious to get ahead as rapidly as possible.

"What's the matter, Owens?" asked all the members of his squad in concert as soon as they were out of the lieutenant's hearing. They were all in the dark, and so was every man belonging to the expedition with the exception of the lieutenant, the sergeant-major and Bob Owens. The latter explained the state of affairs in as few words as he could, and the general verdict was that it would have been no loss to the garrison, or to the service either, if Bristow and his companions had been permitted to depart in peace.

In a few minutes Bob and his men arrived within sight of the place where the horses were staked out, and a hoarse voice broke the stillness. "Halt! Who comes there?" was the challenge.

"Friends, with the countersign," answered Bob after bringing his squad to a halt.

"Advance, one friend, and give the countersign," was the next command.

"Now, boys," said Bob in a low whisper, "you stay here, and when I call out 'Advance, squad,' come up briskly and surround Dodd, so as to be ready to overpower him if he shows the least disposition to resist or cry out."

So saying, Bob moved off in the direction from which the hail sounded, and presently discovered the sentry, who stood at "arms port."

"Halt!" commanded the guard when Bob had approached within a few feet of him. "Give the countersign."

Bob whispered the magic word.

"The countersign is correct," said the sentry, bringing his carbine to a carry.—"It's you, is it, Owens? What's the matter?"

"Advance, squad," said Bob in a low tone. "You haven't seen anything suspicious going on about your post, have you?" he added, wishing to occupy the sentry's attention until his men could come within supporting distance of him. "No? Well, I am sorry to say that there is something suspicious about *you*, and I am ordered to put you in arrest."

He laid hold of the carbine as he said this, and at the same moment two of his men placed their hands upon the sentinel's shoulders. The latter, seeing that resistance was useless, promptly gave up his piece and dropped his hands by his sides. "It's all that Bristow's work," said he in angry tones. "I knew he wouldn't do to tie to."

"Don't say too much," interposed Bob. "You don't want to condemn yourself.—Carey, take this post until relieved."

As Bob marched his squad and his prisoner to the place where he was to meet his commanding officer, he found the intervening posts in the charge of trusty men. Four of the discontented ones had been secured, and it only remained for the lieutenant to perfect arrangements for seizing the others as fast as they came out of the fort. He had already decided upon his plan of operations, and Bob Owens was called upon to take the first step toward carrying it out. After he had listened to some very explicit instructions from his commander, he stole off into the darkness, and, creeping along the outside of the stockade until he reached a point opposite the place where the sentry was posted behind the stables, he stopped and waited to see what was going to happen. About ten feet from him on his left was another soldier, standing upright and motionless in the shadow of the stockade. Ten feet beyond this soldier was another. These were all that Bob could see, but he knew that there were good men and true stationed at regular intervals all along the stockade, waiting to act the several parts that had been assigned to them.

Bob waited and listened for a quarter of an hour or more, and then he heard a conversation carried on in a low tone on the other side of the stockade. He could not catch the words, but he knew that the deserters were beginning to bestir themselves, and that one of their number was talking with the sentry. Presently a scratching, scrambling sound, accompanied by heavy, labored breathing and those incoherent exclamations that men sometimes use when they are exerting themselves to the utmost, told Bob that somebody was making his way up the logs. Keeping his eyes fastened on the top, he saw a soldier climb up and seat himself on the plate. He could see him very plainly against the light background of the sky, and he recognized him at once. It was Bristow. He was about to swing himself off when he discovered Bob standing beneath him. He stopped, peered down into the darkness for a moment, and then called out in a frightened whisper,

"Who is it?"

"It's all right," whispered Bob in reply; "come on."

"Who is it, I say?" repeated Bristow in still more earnest tones.

"Why, don't you know Dodd? Hand me your carbine."

"Oh!" said Bristow with a great sigh of relief. "It *is* all right, isn't it? Here you are."

Holding his carbine by the strap, Bristow passed it down to Bob, who promptly slung it upon his back. The latter then pushed up his sleeves, moved back a little from the stockade, and when Bristow swung himself down by his hands and dropped lightly to the ground, Bob stepped up and took him by the arm.

"I don't need any help," said Bristow, who had landed squarely on his feet. "But I say, Dodd—"

"We'll talk about it as we go along," interrupted Bob. "But not a loud word out of you, unless you want to be gagged."

"Why, good gracious, it's Owens!" gasped Bristow, reeling back against the stockade. He did not ask what Bob was doing there or why he had seized him, for he knew without asking.

"Yes, it is Owens, and the men you saw ride out of the gate with me this afternoon are with me now. Here's one of them," added Bob as a soldier named Loring stepped up and took his place in readiness to catch the next deserter who came over the stockade.

Just then the sentry on the inside placed his mouth close to one of the cracks between the logs and asked, in a cautious tone,

"How is it, Bristow? Is the coast clear?"

"All clear," replied Loring, speaking through the same crack. "Tell the boys to hurry up; we've no time to waste."

If Bob's captive had any idea of attempting to escape or of alarming his companions by crying out, he abandoned it very quickly when he saw the soldiers that were stationed along the stockade. There was a trooper for every deserter, and as fast as the man at the head of the line caught one, another moved up and took his place.

"This bangs me!" said Bristow, in great disgust. "Now comes a court-martial of course, and Goodness only knows what will come after that—the guard-house and a heavy fine, or the military prison at Fort Leavenworth.—I say, Owens, how did the colonel find it out?"

"Do you suppose he tells his secrets to us privates?" asked Bob in reply.

"We spoke to somebody who was not worthy of the confidence we placed in him," continued Bristow. "The thing never could have become known unless one of our own number had proved treacherous. But we can easily find out who he is. There are just thirty of us, and if there are only twenty-nine arrested, the missing man is the guilty one. When I find out who he is, I shall take particular pains to see that the next battle he gets into is his last."

This threat was uttered in a very low tone of voice, for Bristow and his captor had by this time reached the place where the lieutenant had stationed himself to receive his men when they came in with their prisoners. Bob reported, "Your orders have been obeyed, sir," and took his stand close behind his officer.

"I counted only twenty-six," said Bristow when the sergeant-major came up and announced the complete success of the undertaking. "There must be four traitors among us."

"Have you counted in the horse-guards?" asked Bob. "There they are on the top of that ridge."

No, Bristow had not counted them in, for he did not know until that minute that they had been arrested. He was very much astonished when he learned that every one of his party had been secured, and could not for the life of him imagine how the colonel had found out about it; for that he knew *all* about it was evident from the manner in which the arrests had been effected.

Having sent one of his men back to order up the horses, the lieutenant formed his captives in line, threw a guard around them and marched them into the fort. Halting them on the parade, he went in to report to the colonel, and when he came out again he put every one of them into the guard-house; after which Bob and his companions went to the quarters and tumbled into their bunks.

Great was the astonishment among the soldiers the next morning when it became known that the expedition, which they supposed had gone out in search of the hostiles, had returned to the fort and captured thirty armed men, and that the work had been done so quietly that the sentry at the gate never knew anything about it until it was all over. Of course they were quite at a loss to determine who it was that told the colonel about it; and the general impression seemed to be that if there were a traitor among the deserters, he had allowed himself to be captured with the others in order to avoid suspicion.

Among the non-commissioned officers who had attempted to

desert was one of the corporals belonging to Bob's troop, and the next morning Bob was ordered to take his place and do duty as corporal of the guard. He saw the prisoners served with breakfast, and the numerous orders he had to give opened the eyes of one of them, who began to think he had made a discovery. And so he had, but he could not prove it.

"I'll tell you what's a fact, boys," said Bristow as he walked to a remote corner of his prison with a cup of coffee in one hand and some cracker and bacon in the other: "I know whom we have to thank for our arrest."

"Who is it?" asked a dozen voices at once.

"I'd like to send him my compliments in the shape of a bullet from my carbine," said the corporal whose place Bob was then filling. "Tell us who he is, so that we can improve the first chance to get even with him."

"There he is," said Bristow, shaking his piece of cracker at Bob. "He has been trying to get on the blind side of the officers for a long time, as you all know, and he has accomplished his object at last by going back on his comrades."

The prisoners looked at Bob as if they expected him to deny the accusation; but, to the disappointment of some of them who really liked him, he had nothing to say.

"Why don't you speak up and declare that it isn't so?" demanded the corporal.

"Because he dare not," exclaimed Bristow. "He couldn't without telling a lie, and, as he is a good little boy, he wouldn't do that for the world."

"I don't believe he did it," said another of the culprits. "He is not one of us, and how could he have found it out? I believe that the traitor is right here in the guard-house under arrest."

"I know he isn't," declared Bristow. "Bob Owens is the only traitor there is, and you may depend upon it. Now, let me tell you just what is going to happen when the court-martial comes off: it will be proved to the satisfaction of all of you that Owens found out about our plans in some way or other, and went straight to the colonel with them. You will be disrated, Corporal Jim, and Lieutenant Earle, in order to reward Bob for carrying tales and to encourage him to carry more, will give him your place. Why, he has just as good as got the stripes on his arm now."

Corporal Jim looked daggers at Bob, and declared that if he was the one who had disclosed their plot to the colonel, he was too mean for any use, and ought to be drummed out of the fort.

"I promised that if I ever found out who the informer was I would serve him worse than that," said Bristow in savage tones. "I shall keep my promise, too, if I ever get the chance, for I am one who never forgets an injury."

Bob Owens—who, as we know, was not wanting in physical courage—was not at all alarmed by this threat and a good many others like it to which he listened during the fifteen minutes the prisoners were occupied in eating their breakfast. He believed that he was able to take care of No. 1; and when the critical time came, as it did a few weeks later, he proved to the satisfaction of everybody that his confidence in himself was not misplaced.

The court-martial was not long delayed, and the findings being approved by the proper authorities, the sentences were promptly carried out. The culprits were confined in the guard-house for different periods of time, those who had been the most active in inducing their comrades to desert serving a longer sentence than their victims, and fines were imposed upon all of them, Bristow's being by far the heaviest, as he was proved to be the ringleader. He and Gus Robbins—both of whom had been almost constantly in trouble ever since they arrived at the post—were given to understand that if they were detected in another attempt at desertion they could make up their minds to see the inside of the military prison at Fort Leavenworth. Bristow proved to be a first-class prophet. During the progress of the trial it came out that Bob Owens was the one who discovered the plot, and that through him it was communicated to the colonel. Corporal Jim was of course reduced to the ranks, and Bob was promoted to fill the vacancy.

During the next few weeks nothing of interest happened at the fort. The deserters were released as fast as the terms for which they were sentenced expired, some of them penitent and fully resolved to do better in future, while the others were more than ever determined to escape from military control, in spite of all the officers and guards that could be placed around them. They carried out their determination, too, at every opportunity, deserting in parties numbering half a dozen or so, and they generally succeeded in eluding pursuit. It was a singular fact that when the pursuers were commanded by commissioned officers they very often returned without having accomplished anything, but when they were commanded by sergeants or corporals they were almost always successful. Luck was on the side of the "non-coms," and the colonel finally learned to put a great deal of confidence in them. Bob Owens was particularly fortunate in this respect, and that was the reason his superior sent for him one morning after the officer of the day had reported that seven men had deserted during the previous night, taking their arms and a supply of ammunition with them.

CHAPTER IV

A PERILOUS UNDERTAKING

"Corporal," said the commandant, taking off his eye-glasses with a jerk, as he always did when he was about to say something emphatic, "there are the names of seven men who deserted last night. I want you to take command of a squad and follow them up and arrest them."

"Very good, sir," replied Bob.

"I don't know which way they went, or anything about it," continued the colonel. "That is something you will have to find out for yourself. I *do* know, however, that they went on foot, and that they are armed and well supplied with ammunition. I want you to capture them at all hazards—at all hazards, I say," repeated the colonel, bringing his open hand down upon the table with a ringing slap. "If you come back without them you need not offer any excuses, for I shall not listen to them. Arrest anybody you catch outside the stockade wearing a United States uniform, no matter who he is. There have been no passes granted this morning, and no one except the guards and the officer of the day has any business outside. That's all."

Bob saluted and hurried from the room. As he passed

through the hall he glanced at the list he held in his hand, and saw that it was headed by the names of Bristow and Gus Robbins.

"This is about the easiest job I have had yet, and these fellows are just as good as captured already," said he to himself. "I know right where to look for them, and I wouldn't be in their shoes for all the money the paymaster had in his safe the last time he was here. They are booked for Leavenworth, sure.—May I go out, Willis?" he asked of the sentry at the gate; "I am acting under orders."

"That's all right," was the reply; "the officer of the day told me to pass you. You are going after those deserters, I suppose? Well, now, look here," added the sentry, after looking all around to make sure that there was no officer in sight: "you remember those mulewhackers who brought that freight here the other day, don't you? Well, Bristow and the rest have gone off to join them. I am certain of it, for I heard Bristow talking with them, and they assured him that the wagon-master would give him steady work and good wages if he would hire out to him. Bristow didn't hesitate to talk with them about it in the presence of a dozen of us."

"That was only a ruse on his part," said Bob confidently. "If I followed the trail of those teamsters I should have my trouble for my pains. I am going as straight toward Brownsville as I can go, and I shall have my hand on Mr. Bristow's collar before I have gone thirty miles. You may rest assured that I shall not come back without him, for if I do I don't know what the colonel will say to me."

Bob hastened toward the place where the horses were picketed, and there he found the officer of the day and the six picked men who had been detailed to accompany him. It was the work of but a few minutes to lead their horses into the fort and put the saddles and bridles on them; and when this had been done, and Bob and his men had secured their carbines, sabres and revolvers and put two days' rations in their haversacks, they mounted and rode through the gate at a sharp trot. They were quiet and orderly enough as long as they remained within sight of the fort, but when the first ridge over which they passed shut them out from view they abandoned their efforts to keep in column, threw off all restraint and shouted and sang at the top of their voices. They looked upon an expedition like this as a "lark," and enjoyed it as much as a schoolboy enjoys a picnic.

Bob did not stop at the first ranches he passed, for he knew that the deserters (provided, of course, that they had fled along that trail) must have gone by them in the night, and that consequently their inmates could give him no information. Besides, Bob had learned by experience that there was very little confidence to be placed in anything the ranchemen might say regarding a deserter. A good many of them had served in the army during the war, and, knowing how very hard is the life a soldier leads, they sympathized with him in his efforts to escape, and aided him by every means in their power. Where there was one farmer or stock-raiser who would give a squad like Bob's any information that could be relied on, there were a dozen who would conceal the deserter in their houses and send his pursuers off on the wrong trail.

After Bob and his troopers had ridden about fifteen miles, and had shouted and sung off a little of their surplus enthusiasm, they relapsed into silence and settled down to business. They halted on the top of every ridge to survey the country before them, and called at every ranche that lay along their route; but nothing was to be seen or heard of Bristow and his party. About noon they came within sight of a squatter's cabin, and Bob decided to stop there and eat dinner. The owner of the cabin was at home, and he welcomed the horsemen with every appearance of cordiality.

"Alight an' hitch, strangers," said he, when he had succeeded in quieting the small army of dogs which came out from under the cabin to dispute the further advance of the troopers. "You're as welcome as the flowers in May."

"Thank you," said Bob as he swung himself from his saddle. "We intend to stop here and rest for an hour or so. We'll boil our coffee and cook our rations on your stove, if you have no objections."

"I ain't got no stove," replied the squatter hastily— "leastways, none that you can do cookin' on," he added, with some confusion, when he saw Bob and one or two of his men look up at the stovepipe which projected above the roof.

"All right!" replied the corporal, silencing by a look one of the troopers who was about to say something. "Then we shall have to build a fire outside; but that will do just as well, for we are used to cooking our grub in that way.—Now, Carey, if you and Loring will skirmish around and find some wood and start the coffee-pot going, we will look out for your nags."

"Corporal," whispered one of the troopers, "there's a bug under that chip. In other words, this old rascal has some reason for wishing to keep us out of his cabin."

"Say nothing out loud," replied Bob with a warning gesture. "We are on the right track, and I know it. If we fail now, it will be through our own blundering."

Having seen the horses staked out, Bob walked back to the cabin, and found the squatter in conversation with Carey and

Loring. His first words indicated that he had been trying to pump them, but without success.

"Say, soldier, where might you be a-travellin' to?" he asked as Bob came up. "I asked them two fellows, an' they told me I had better ask you."

"We are looking for seven deserters who passed this way some time this morning," answered Bob. "They were on foot and carried carbines. Seen anything of such a party?"

The squatter brought his hands together with a loud slap before he replied.

"I jest knowed them fellows wasn't what they allowed they was," said he. "In course I seed 'em, an' they told me they was a-lookin' for deserters themselves. They went off that way, toward the old Brazos trail," added the squatter, pointing in a direction which lay exactly at right angles with the course Bob had been pursuing.

"Did they?" exclaimed the corporal with a great show of eagerness. "Thank you for the information. We will go that way too as soon as we have eaten dinner. How long ago did they pass this way?"

"Jest at daylight."

"That's another lie," said Bob to himself. "They didn't desert until after midnight, and they couldn't have travelled between fifteen and twenty miles in less than five hours on foot. An infantryman might do it on a pinch, but a trooper couldn't."

"You'll have to hurry up if you want to ketch 'em," continued the squatter, who seemed to grow nervous when he saw how deliberately the troopers went about their preparations for dinner. "They was a-lumberin' along right peart."

"Oh, there's no need that we should throw ourselves into a perspiration," replied Bob indifferently. "We don't care if we don't find them for a week. You see, when we are out on an expedition like this we are not obliged to drill, and our pay goes on just the same. If you have anything good to eat, trot it out; we're wealthy."

But the squatter protested that he had nothing in his cabin except bacon and crackers, and his supply of these necessary articles was so small that he could not possibly spare any of it. He said so much on this point that the troopers would have been dull indeed if they had not suspected something.

"He wants to get us away from here, doesn't he?" said Carey as soon as he had a chance to speak to Bob. "He thinks that if he provides us with a good dinner we will spend a long time in eating it. Now, corporal, I will bet you anything you please that—"

"I know," interrupted Bob, "and I want you to take a look into the matter at once. This is my plan."

Here Bob whispered some rapid instructions to the trooper, who winked first one eye and then the other to show that he understood them. Pulling his pipe from his pocket, he proceeded to fill it with tobacco, while Bob walked up to the squatter, and, taking him confidentially by the arm, said, as he led him out of earshot of the men, who had seated themselves about the fire,

"May I have a word with you in private? You see, I am an officer, and it won't do for me to talk too freely in the presence of those I command."

So saying, Bob led the squatter behind the cabin and began making some very particular inquiries concerning Bristow and his party: What sort of looking fellows were they? What did they say? Did they get anything to eat at the cabin? and did his friend the squatter really think they had gone toward the old Brazos trail? The man was very uneasy, and seemed impatient to go back to the fire again; but by holding fast to his arm, and plying him with such questions as these, Bob managed to keep him behind the cabin for about five minutes, and that was long enough for Carey to carry out the orders that had been given him.

As soon as Bob and the squatter disappeared around the corner of the cabin, Carey put his pipe into his mouth, and, enjoining silence upon his comrades by shaking his fore finger at them, he quickly mounted the steps that led to the porch and walked into the cabin. As he did so there was a faint rustling in one corner of the room, and, looking over his left shoulder without turning his head, Carey saw a man who was lying on a rude couch draw a blanket quickly over his face. In his eagerness to conceal his features the man probably forgot that he had a pair of feet, for he pulled the blanket up a little too high.

"Aha! my fine lad," said the trooper as he noiselessly opened the stove-door and looked into it, as if he were searching for a live coal with which to light his pipe, "I see a pair of No. 12 army brogans, and also the lower portions of a pair of light blue breeches with a yellow stripe down the seams. Bryant, my boy, that's you. I see also that this stove is in perfect order, but as there are no coals in it, I'll have to get a light at the fire outside."

When Carey came out of the cabin his comrades' faces were full of inquiry, but the trooper only winked at them and nodded his head, as if to say that he could tell something that would astonish them if he only felt so disposed.

By this time dinner was ready, and Loring's loud call of "Coffee!" brought Bob and the squatter from behind the cabin. The latter accepted Loring's invitation to drink a cup of coffee with "the boys," but he disposed of it in great haste, hot as it was, as if he hoped by his example to induce them to do likewise. But Bob and his companions were in no hurry. They lingered a long time over their homely meal, and then the smokers were allowed to empty a pipe apiece before the order was given to "catch up." The squatter began to breathe easier after that, and when he saw the troopers in their saddles and ready to start, his delight was so apparent that they all noticed it.

"Wa'l, good-bye, if you must go," said he cheerily. "Will you stop when you come back?"

"Oh, you needn't expect to see us here again," said Bob. "If we go to Brazos City, we shall take a short cut across the country when we return to the fort."

"That's where I reckon they're goin', as I told you; an' my advice would be for you to go straight to Brazos, without stoppin' on the way, an' when they get there you'll be all ready to take 'em in. See?"

"Yes, I see," answered Bob, "and it's something worth thinking of.—Forward, column left! Trot! gallop!"

The troopers moved rapidly away from the cabin, and, to the intense surprise and indignation of all his followers, who thought that their corporal had been deceived by the squatter, Bob led them off toward the old Brazos trail. At length one of them ventured to remonstrate.

"Corporal," said he, "you're going wrong."

"I know it," answered Bob.—"Carey, tell us what you saw in that cabin. Were our suspicions correct?"

"Indeed they were," was Carey's reply. "In the first place, that stove was all right, but the squatter didn't want us to use it, for Bryant was hiding in the cabin. He was lying on the floor, covered up with a blanket."

"How do you know it was Bryant?" asked Bob. "Did you see his face?"

"No, I didn't; it was concealed by the blanket. I saw his feet," said Carey; and his answer was received by the troopers with a sigh of satisfaction. It was all that was needed to establish the identity of the man who had taken refuge in the squatter's cabin.

"I didn't think I could be wrong," observed Bob, "for that man condemned himself before we had been in his presence ten minutes."

"Why don't you go back and snatch Bryant?" demanded one of the troopers, seeing that the corporal did not slacken his pace. "Why didn't you do it while we were at the cabin?"

"Because I had no right to do it," answered Bob. "If I should go to searching houses, I might get myself into trouble with the colonel. Another thing, boys: I shouldn't care to enter that man's castle to look for anything unless I was a civil officer and armed with a search-warrant. He is a hard one, unless his looks belie him."

"I thought so myself," said Loring. "But you are not going back without Bryant, are you? What do you suppose he is doing there, anyway?"

"Of course I shall not go back without him," answered Bob quietly. "He has probably hired out to that squatter, and we must watch our chance and catch him out of doors before we can arrest him."

"Well, are you going to Brazos City?"

"Not by a long shot. Bristow and the fellows who are still with him have not gone that way. As soon as we get behind that belt of post-oaks you see in advance of us, I intend to circle around and go back toward the river again."

Although the troopers rode at a rapid gait, it took them nearly three hours to carry out this programme. At the end of that time they struck the old stage-road, which, in the days gone by, had served as a highway between Brownsville and some of the remote frontier-towns; but when the raiders forced the settlements back into the interior the stage-route was abandoned, and all that now remained to tell of the business that had once been done on it were the half-ruined stations which were scattered along the road at intervals of fifteen or twenty miles.

These stations were built of stone, and were large enough to accommodate a dozen horses and half as many stable-men and drivers, besides the necessary food for both men and animals. Each station was provided with a "dug-out," a miniature fort, into which the employees of the route could retreat in case they were attacked by hostile Indians or Mexican raiders. It was simply a cellar of sufficient size to shelter nine or ten men at close quarters, covered with logs and dirt, and furnished with loopholes on all sides at the height of a foot or more above the ground. It looked like a mound of earth supported on logs about two feet high. The only way of getting into one of these little fortifications was through an underground passage-way which led from the stables. With these arrangements for their defence a few well-armed and determined men could hold their own against all the raiders that could get around them.

About four o'clock in the afternoon Bob and his troopers came within sight of one of these stations, and as soon as their eyes rested upon it they drew up their horses with a jerk, at the same time uttering exclamations of astonishment and delight. Standing in front of the open door were several men dressed in the uniform of the regular army. They seemed to be holding a consultation, and so deeply engrossed were they with their deliberations that they did not notice the approach of the troopers, although the latter had stopped their horses on the summit of a high ridge in plain view of them.

"I wonder if those are our men?" said Carey, with some excitement in his tones.

"We shall soon know," was Bob's calm reply. "Whoever they are, they will have to give an account of themselves, for I am instructed to arrest everybody I meet wearing a uniform."

"If they *are* our fellows, we've got them corralled," remarked Loring.

"Yes, but I don't much like the way we have 'corralled' them," returned Carey. "Do you see that dug-out about twenty yards from the northwest corner of the station? If they go in there they can laugh at us. The only way we could get them out would be to starve them out."

"That would take too long," said Bob; and the tone in which the words were uttered made his comrades look at him with some curiosity. "Let's go down there and interview them, and then we shall know how to act. Forward! Trot!"

Just as these commands were given a commotion among the men in front of the station indicated that somebody had sounded an alarm. They gazed at the troopers for a moment as if they were thunderstruck, and then made a simultaneous rush for the entrance. This action on their part told Bob as plainly as words that they were the men of whom he had been sent in pursuit, and that they did not intend to go back to the fort if they could help it. A moment later a loud slamming and pounding indicated that the deserters were trying to close and barricade the door. This had scarcely been accomplished when the troopers dashed up to the station and swung themselves out of their saddles.

Leaving two of his men to hold the horses, Bob and the rest walked around the corner of the station and looked at the dug-out. There was a face in front of every loophole. Anybody could see that the deserters had the advantage of position, and the troopers wondered what Bob was going to do about it. They glanced at his face, but could see nothing there to tell them whether he was excited, afraid or discouraged. It wore its usual expression.

"Well, boys," said Bob at length, "if you have grown tired of roaming about the country, come out, and we will go back to the post. The colonel wants to see you."

"We don't doubt it, but we don't want to see him," replied a voice that Bob recognized at once. "We think we see ourselves going back! We didn't desert for that."

"Gus Robbins, I am sorry that you are in there," said Bob. "What will you say to your father and mother when you see them again?"

"Don't know, I am sure," answered Gus. "Haven't had any time to think about that. But you know yourself that I can't go back to the post. The colonel said that if I were ever court-marshaled again for desertion, I should go to prison; but I'll fight till I drop before I'll do that."

"Say, Bob," shouted another voice, "do you remember what I said I would do to that informer if I ever found out who he was? You are the fellow, and here's your pay."

It was Bristow who spoke, and as he uttered these words he thrust the muzzle of his carbine through the loophole in front of him. The chorus of ejaculations and remonstrances which arose from the inside of the dug-out showed that the rest of the deserters were not yet ready to resort to the use of their firearms; but Bristow was almost half crazed by rage and fear, and just as somebody seized him from behind and jerked him away from the loophole, his carbine roared, and Bob Owens turned halfway round and staggered back a step or two, as if he were struck and about to fall.

This unexpected act excited Bob's troopers—with whom he was an especial favorite—almost to frenzy. Believing that he had been seriously if not fatally injured—it did not seem possible that anybody could miss a mark of the size of his body at the distance of ten paces—one of them sprang forward to support him, while the others discharged their carbines at the loopholes in rapid succession. Their volley was not entirely without effect, for a loud yell of agony came from the inside of the dug-out, bearing testimony to the fact that one bullet at least had found a target somewhere on the person of one of the deserters.

"Cease firing!" shouted Bob.

He gently released himself from the embrace of the strong

arms that had been thrown around him, and looked down at the gaping rent Bristow's bullet had made in the breast of his coat. The missile had passed through his thick carbine-sling and breast-belt, had cut into his coat, vest and shirt, and ploughed a deep furrow through a well-filled wallet which he carried in his inside pocket. Fortunately, it was a glancing shot, but the force with which it struck him was almost sufficient to knock him off his feet.

"I'm not hurt at all," said he as his men crowded about him, "but I shall have to put a patch on my coat when I get back to the post.—I say, there," he shouted, addressing himself to the inmates of the dug-out, "was there anybody hurt in there? I thought I heard a yell."

"Yes, and you'll hear another yell if you don't go away and let us alone," replied Bristow. "I'll make a better shot the next time I pull on you."

"All right!" said Bob. "I'll give you a chance in just about five minutes.—Loring," he added in a lower tone, "you and Phillips stay here and hold the horses, and the rest of you follow me."

"Are you going to storm them?" asked Loring.

"I am," was the decided reply. "It is the only way I can get them out, for they'll not come of their own free will."

"Then I sha'n't stay here and hold the horses; that's flat," declared Loring.

"Neither will I," chimed in Phillips. "The picket-pins will hold them as well as we can."

"All right!" replied Bob. "Stake them out, and while you are doing it Carey and I will see how we are going to get into the station."

The door to which Bob now turned his attention did not prove to be a very serious obstacle. It was made of heavy planks, and if it had been in good condition it would have taken a good deal of chopping with a sharp axe before one could have forced his way through it; but the hinges had rusted off, and the planks had shrunk to such a degree that the bar which held the door in its place could be seen and reached with a sabre. A few blows with one of these weapons knocked this bar from its place, and when that was done, the door, having nothing to support it, fell back into the stable with a loud crash. Bob entered, with Carey at his heels, and, making his way to a small apartment which had once been used as a sleeping-room by the stable-men and drivers, he found there a trap-door, which he threw open, revealing a flight of rude steps leading into the underground passage that communicated with the dug-out. By this time the rest of the troopers arrived on the scene. They looked dubiously at the dark passage-way, and then they looked at Bob.

"Do you really mean to go down there, Owens?" asked Loring. "It's sure death."

"I believe so myself, but I am going all the same," replied Bob, who was thoroughly aroused by the attempt that had been made on his life. "If we are not willing to face death at any moment, we had no business to enlist. Must I go alone?"

"Not much," was the unanimous response. "If you are bound to go, we are going too."

"Leave your sabres and carbines here," commanded Bob. "They will only be in the way. Draw revolvers, but don't shoot except in self-defence."

Bob knew as well as his men did that he was about to enter upon a very perilous undertaking. Bristow had shown that he was desperate enough to shoot, and he had even threatened that if he got another chance at Bob he would make a better shot than he did before. Some of the men who were with him were known to be hard characters, and it was very probable that they would back him up in the resistance he seemed determined to make. But Bob, having made up his mind as to the course he ought pursue, never once faltered. He was a soldier, and a soldier's first duty was to obey orders. He had been commanded to find the deserters and arrest them at all hazards; and, having obeyed the first part of his instructions, he was resolved to carry them out to the letter or perish in the attempt.

"Now I think we are all ready," said Bob, after the sabres and carbines had been laid in the empty bunks and the revolvers drawn and examined. "Stick close to me, and remember that if we don't take them they will kill us. Bristow, Sandy and Talbot are the only men we have to fear, and if we can only get the drop on them we are all right. Come on."

Although Bob was the youngest soldier, he was the calmest one of the seven troopers who descended those steps. When he reached the bottom he looked along the passage-way toward the dug-out, which was dimly lighted by the sunbeams which streamed in through the loopholes on the western side, and saw the deserters standing in line awaiting his approach.

"Halt!" cried a voice. "Come a step nearer and you are all dead men."

It was Bristow who spoke, and the words were followed by the ominous click of the lock of his carbine.

CHAPTER V

THE NEW SCOUT

"Halt!" cried Bristow again. It was so dark in the passage-way that he could not see the troopers, but the sound of their footsteps told him that they were still advancing toward the dug-out. "That's twice," he continued. "If I have to halt you the third time, I'll send a bullet out there."

"Bristow, you had better not try that," answered Bob, without the least tremor in his voice. "You have already done more than you will want to stand punishment for. Besides, I have got you covered, and if you move that carbine a hair's breadth you are a gone deserter."

"And I've got the drop on you, Sandy," said Carey, thrusting his cocked revolver over Bob's shoulder, "so don't wink.—I say, corporal," he added in a whisper, "I don't see Talbot anywhere."

"Neither do I," answered Bob. "Keep your eyes open, for he may be up to playing us some trick."

Whether it was the cool determination exhibited by Bob and his men, or the consciousness that they were in the wrong that took all the fight out of the deserters, we cannot tell; but they were cowed by something, and when Corporal Owens and his troopers filed into the dug-out, and the former sternly commanded them to "throw up," every carbine was dropped to the ground and five pairs of hands were raised in the air.

"Where's the other?" demanded Bob. "There ought to be six of you."

"Here I am," said a faint voice.

Bob looked in the direction from which the voice came, and saw Talbot sitting in a dark corner, his carbine lying by his side and both his hands raised above his head. He wore a handkerchief around his forehead, and, dim as the light was, Bob could see that it was streaked with blood.

"Are you badly hurt?" he asked with some anxiety.

"No, he isn't," exclaimed Bristow, before the wounded man could speak. "A glancing ball cut a little crease in his scalp, and he thinks he is killed."

"I wish you had this little crease in your own scalp," said Talbot, looking savagely at Bristow. "If it hadn't been for you I never should have been here."

"And if it hadn't been for *you*, and a few cowards just like you, we never should have been captured," retorted Bristow. "We could have held our own against a squad four times as big as the one Owens has brought with him; but now—"

"That'll do," interrupted Bob. "I am not going to have any quarrelling here; and, Bristow, there's a court-martial coming, and you had better keep a quiet tongue in your head.—Carey, stand in the mouth of that passage-way.—Phillips, pick up the carbines, and the rest of you sound them."

These orders were promptly obeyed, and when the "sounding" had been completed the deserters had not even a pocket-knife left.

"Now, boys," continued Bob, "as you seem to like these quarters so well, you can stay here to-night—all except you, Talbot; you will come up and have your wound examined. We didn't come prepared to take care of injured men, but we will do the best we can for you.—We will get some supper for you men, and when you feel so inclined you can spread your blankets on the floor and go to sleep.—Go on, Carey."

At a sign from Bob the troopers followed Carey, who led the way along the passage; then Talbot fell in, carrying his blanket over his shoulder, and Bob brought up the rear. The trap-door was shut, and Talbot was informed that the sleeping-room was to be his prison for the night. His wound was dressed with some cold coffee that Bob happened to have in his canteen, and the deserter was assured that there was no cause for apprehension. The wound, which was scarcely an inch long, was only skin-deep, but it bled profusely, and that was probably the reason why Talbot was so badly frightened. When two sentries had been posted— one at the door of the stable to keep an eye on Talbot, and the other at the dug-out to see that the deserters who were confined there did not attempt to work their way out during the night—Bob ordered supper to be served at once. He had performed a brave act, and now that the danger was over he began to realize that he had passed through something of an ordeal. He lifted his cap, and found that his forehead was covered with great drops of perspiration.

"You have done well," said Carey, extending his hand to Bob when the latter came out of the sleeping-room. "I didn't know you had so much pluck. I shall take particular pains to see that the lieutenant hears of this day's work."

"He will tell you that I did nothing but my duty," replied Bob, who was very glad to know that his men were satisfied with his conduct.

"But it isn't everybody who is brave enough to do his duty," said Carey as he touched a match to the light-wood he had piled in the fireplace; "and perhaps the lieutenant will say that you ought to be a sergeant. That *was* Bryant back there in that squatter's cabin, wasn't it? I looked for him the minute we entered the dug-out."

"So did I," answered Bob, "and I saw at a glance that he wasn't there. We will attend to him to-morrow."

"But perhaps he won't be there."

"I think he will. It is my opinion that he has hired out to that squatter, and that he intends to trust to disguise to escape recognition. A man in citizen's clothes doesn't look much like the same man in uniform; did you ever notice that? But even if he isn't there, what odds does it make to us? We are having a good time, and I would just as soon stay out here on the plains for a week or ten days as to go back to the fort and drill."

"I say, corporal," exclaimed the sentry who was stationed at the door, "here's somebody coming, and unless my eyes are going back on me he is dressed in uniform."

"Who in the world can it be?" exclaimed Carey.

"We'll soon find out," replied Bob, "for if he has got any of our uncle's clothes on we are bound to take him in, unless he proves to be an officer."

Bob and his men hurried to the door, and, looking in the

direction in which the sentry was gazing, saw a horseman about a quarter of a mile away. He had halted on the top of a ridge, and Loring, who had good "Plains eyes," declared that he was looking at them through a field-glass. He certainly was dressed in uniform, and had with him a small black mule which bore a good-sized pack on its back.

"I can't make him out," said Bob, waving his hand in the air and beckoning the horseman to approach. "He is a soldier, but what is he doing with that pack-mule? It isn't Bryant, is it? If it is, where did he get that mule and that field-glass?— Loring, you and Phillips put the bridles on your horses— never mind the saddles—and stand by to give him a race if he tries to run away. Don't mount until I give the word."

But the horseman had no intention of running away. He replied to Bob's signal by waving his hand over his head, and after putting away his field-glass rode down the ridge and came toward the station at a gallop. As he approached nearer the troopers saw that he was a stranger, and a very good-looking one, too. He was almost as dark as an Indian, his hair was long enough to reach to his shoulders, and the eyes that looked out from under the peak of his fatigue-cap were as black as midnight and as sharp as those of an eagle. He rode a magnificent horse, and his seat was easy and graceful. His only weapon—that is, the only one that could be seen—was a heavy Winchester rifle, which was slung at his back. If he was a soldier, he was a very fancy one, for his cavalry uniform, although in strict keeping with the regulations, was made of the finest material; he wore white gauntlet gloves on his hands; and instead of the ungainly, ill-fitting army shoe he wore fine boots, the heels of which were armed with small silver spurs. The troopers thought from his dress and carriage that he must be an officer, and when he drew rein in front of the station they stood at "attention" and saluted him.

"I don't deserve that honor, boys," said the stranger with a laugh; "I am not a shoulder-strap."

"You are not?" exclaimed Bob, who was not a little astonished as well as provoked at the mistake he had made. "Well, it seems to me that you are throwing on a good many frills for a private. Where do you belong?"

"At Fort Lamoine," said the stranger; and the answer was given in a tone quite as curt as was that in which the question was asked.

"So do I, but I don't remember to have seen you there, and so I shall have to ask you to give an account of yourself. Dismount."

"I shall do as I please about that," replied the stranger, who had all the while been staring very hard at Bob.

"Well, you won't do as you please about it," returned the corporal, while Carey walked up and took the stranger's horse by the bit. "You will do as *I* please. If you belong at Fort Lamoine you will go there with me in the morning, and then I shall be sure you get there. I am acting under orders."

The horseman thrust his hand into the inside pocket of his jacket, and pulling out a bill-book took from it a paper which he opened and handed to Bob to read.

"If you are acting under orders I have no more to say," said he, "but there is something which I think will see me through until day after to-morrow. It is my furlough. Look here, partner," he added suddenly, "isn't your name Bob Owens?"

The latter started as if he had been shot, his under jaw dropped down, and for a few seconds he stood looking at the speaker as if he could hardly believe his ears. Then a light seemed to break in upon him, and springing forward he grasped the horseman by the arm and fairly pulled him out of the saddle. After that he shook one of his hands with both his own and executed a sort of war-dance around him, while the troopers stood and looked on in speechless amazement.

"George Ackerman, I am delighted to see you again," cried Bob as soon as he could speak. "I take it all back, George: I didn't mean to insult you."

"It's Owens, isn't it?" said George, for it was he.

"Of course it is; and if you hadn't been blind you would have known it as soon as you saw me," replied Bob.

"I don't think my eyesight is any worse than your own, for you didn't know me until I called you by name," retorted George. "Your uniform tells me where you have been and what you have been doing since I last saw you, but it doesn't tell me how I came to lose you in Galveston so suddenly and mysteriously. If we had kept together a little while longer we should have been all right, for I had scarcely missed you before I ran against Mr. Gilbert—the friend to whom I wrote for money, you know. If you belong at Fort Lamoine, what are you doing here?"

"Stake out your horse and mule and I will tell you all about it," answered Bob. "But first tell me what right you have to wear those clothes."

"I am a United States scout," replied George. "At least, that was the title under which I was sworn in, but it does not clearly explain the duties that are expected of me. I am to act as guide to the troops when they cross the river in pursuit of the raiders."

"Oh yes," exclaimed Bob; "I remember all about it now. I was off after the hostiles when you came to the post and offered your services to the colonel. When I came back I found that the men had a good deal to say about our new scout, who, they said, looked about as much like a scout as they looked like the queen of England; but I had no idea who he was; and, seeing it's you, I'll not arrest you," he added with a laugh.—"Great Caesar! that was the second close call I have had to-day."

"If I had had any idea that you were going to touch him I should have warned you," said George. "It won't do for a stranger to come within reach of him, and it's the greatest wonder in the world that he didn't knock your brains out."

While the two friends were talking, George Ackerman, with the dexterity acquired by long experience, relieved the mule of his heavy pack and slipped the halter over his head, leaving the animal at liberty. Bob, judging the mule by those unruly members of his species that were employed in the quartermaster's department at the fort, stepped up and attempted to lay hold of his foretop; but the animal dodged him very cleverly, and, wheeling like lightning, sent both his heels at the boy's head. The latter dropped just in time to escape the blow, but he felt the "wind" of the heels in his face and heard them whistle close by his ear.

"Does he always act that way when strangers approach him?" asked Bob as he picked up his cap. "If he does, you need not be afraid that anybody will steal him. I tried to catch him because I was afraid he would run off."

"Oh, he'll not do that. I never think of staking him out, for he always stays by my horse, and I can catch him anywhere. There's a horse for you, Bob, and the best one I ever owned. He is a present from Mr. Gilbert, who bought him in

Kentucky for his own private use, but when he found that I was going into the army he gave him to me, with the assurance that Fletcher and his band could never make a prisoner of me while I was on his back. I lost my old horse, Ranger, at the time I was captured by the Greasers, and he was killed at the battle of Queretaro. Now, what are you doing so far away from the fort?" asked George as he picked up his picket-pin and led the horse around the station to find a good place to stake him out. "How did you come to go into the army, anyway, and what have you been doing to win those stripes?"

"It would take a long time to answer your last two questions," answered Bob, "and so we will leave them until the rest of the boys have gone to bed. I came here in pursuit of seven men who deserted last night."

"You did? Well, Bob, your superiors must have a good deal of confidence in you to send you off on such an expedition. Where do you expect to find them?"

"I have found them already, and arrested them too; that is, I have caught six of them, and I know where the other one is. I intend to take him in hand to-morrow, though, to tell the truth, I don't know just how I am going to do it. I could have arrested him to-day if I had had authority to take him out of a house; but I wasn't sure on that point, and so I let him go until I could have time to make up my mind to something. I got *that* about fifteen minutes before you came up," said Bob, directing his friend's attention to the hole in his coat that had been made by Bristow's bullet. "My men returned the fire and slightly wounded one of the deserters, who is now laid out on his blanket in the sleeping-room. By the way, do you know Gus Robbins?"

"I should say I did," replied George, after he had followed

the course of the bullet through Bob's clothing and expressed his surprise at his friend's narrow escape. "He ran away from his home in Foxboro', and came down here to visit my cousin, who was at that time living with his father at my ranche. He and Ned, who were constantly pluming themselves on the numerous scrapes from which they had narrowly escaped, could not rest easy until they kicked up a row in the settlement, and they did it by shooting Mr. Cook's cattle. The consequence was, that I had to show them the way out of the country. Don't you remember I told you all about it on the morning we walked from that trapper's cabin to White River Landing? I say, Bob, have you any idea of becoming a trapper when your term of service expires?"

"Nary idea," was the emphatic reply. "A soldier's life is hard enough for me, and there is quite as much danger in it as I care to face."

"What do you know about Gus Robbins?" continued George. "He left my cousin Ned very suddenly in Brownsville, and none of us ever heard of him afterward. It can't be possible that he enlisted too?"

"Yes, he did. He belongs to my troop, and is just as fond of getting into scrapes as he ever was. When he is not in the guard-house he is almost sure to be doing extra duty for some offence against military discipline. He was one of the deserters I was ordered to capture, and he is in the dug-out now. But I almost wish he had got away. You know him, and when I was arresting him I almost felt as if I were doing something against you. I haven't forgotten that you offered me a home, and—"

"The obligation is all on my side," interrupted George. "You saved my life twice. Let's sit down here and talk a while. Go ahead and tell me something."

The boys threw themselves on the grass near the place where George had staked out his horse, and Bob began and described some of the interesting incidents that had happened since he last saw the cub pilot. He told the truth in regard to everything, not even excepting the parting in Galveston. His experience in the army was rapidly working a change in him, and he had not told a wilful lie since he assured the recruiting-officer that he was an orphan and that there was no one in the world who had a right to say whether he should enlist or not.

"I have done a good many mean things in my life, I am sorry to say," Bob added in winding up his story, "but about the meanest trick I ever played upon anybody I played upon you on the day we parted. I found fifty cents in my watch-pocket, which I had carelessly shoved in there when money was plenty, and I knew it would buy me supper and lodging. It wasn't enough for both of us, so I ran away from you and went off by myself. That's the way we became separated, and I tell you of it at the risk of losing your friendship."

"You risk nothing at all," replied George, extending his hand. "I couldn't expect that you would take care of me and pay my way at the sacrifice of all your own personal comfort; but I do wish you had waited just a little longer, for then you never would have had to enlist. I am ready to prove that I think as much of you now as I ever did. I shall keep an eye on you until your term of service expires, and then you must go home with me. I am sole master there now—Mr. Gilbert is my guardian, but he never has a word to say—and as you have no home of your own—"

"That was a lie, George," interrupted Bob. "I have a home at Rochdale, a few miles below Linwood, where I first pulled you out of the river—you know where it is—and as kind a father and mother as any scoundrel of my size ever had.

When I ran away I intended to drop my identity altogether, and that was the reason I told you I was alone in the world. What do you think of me *now*?"

George was greatly astonished at this confession, for he had put implicit faith in Bob's story. He was strictly truthful himself, and he could not understand how a boy as physically brave as Bob Owens had showed himself to be could be coward enough to tell a lie.

"I feel sorry for you," said he at length; "and if I were in your place I would go home as soon as I received my discharge—if you keep on as you have begun you may rest assured that it will be an honorable one—and try to make amends for my misdeeds. Remember that

'No star is ever lost we once have seen;
We always may be what we might have been,'

and go resolutely to work to 'live it down.' You've got the pluck to do it, I know."

"Coffee!" shouted Carey, thrusting his head around the corner of the station.

"By the way," continued George as he and Bob arose to their feet, "what did you mean by saying that, seeing it was I, you wouldn't arrest me?"

"Oh, the colonel was mad when he started me out this morning, and ordered me to gobble up everybody—that is, privates and non-commissioned officers—I caught outside the stockade. But of course I couldn't touch you if I wanted to, for your leave of absence protects you. You will stay here to-night and ride to the fort with us to-morrow, will you not?"

"Certainly I will. Having found you again, I am not going to leave you in a hurry. Say, Bob, would you have any objections to bringing Gus Robbins up to eat supper with us?"

"None whatever. I am sorry to be obliged to keep him and the rest so closely confined, but I know that they are a slippery lot—every one of them has deserted before—and if I should let them get away now that I have got a grip on them, the colonel would give me Hail Columbia. Gus has got himself into a mess, George. The first time he deserted he was simply put into the guard-house and fined, but this escapade is going to land him at Leavenworth. Now I will make you acquainted with our boys, and then I will go down and tell Gus that you want to see him."

After the new scout had been introduced to the troopers, Bob raised the trap-door and descended into the dug-out, while George opened his pack-saddle and took out of it a tin cup and plate, a can of condensed milk, a box or two of sardines and a few other delicacies, which he laid upon the table beside the simple fare that Carey had just served up. By the time he had finished the work of opening the cans with the aid of a formidable-looking hunting-knife which he drew from his boot-leg, Bob returned, followed by a soldier who looked so unlike the dashing, fashionably-dressed Gus Robbins he had seen in company with his cousin Ned that George could hardly bring himself to believe that he was the same boy. He looked pale and haggard; and that was not to be wondered at, for the prison at Fort Leavenworth was constantly looming up before him.

George, as we know, had a very slight acquaintance with Gus Robbins, having passed only a few hours in his company, and he was under no obligations whatever to interest himself in his behalf; but when he saw how utterly miserable he was, his heart bled for him, and he at once hit upon a plan for getting him out of the trouble he had brought upon himself. He greeted Gus very cordially, gave him a seat beside himself at the table, and tried to put a little life into him by talking about almost everything except life in the army.

The deserters must have thought that their captors felt very much elated over their success, for a noisier party than that which was gathered about that rough board table was never seen anywhere. Being almost entirely free from military restraint—sergeants and corporals do not hold their men with so tight a rein as the commissioned officers do, although they exact just as prompt obedience to their commands—they told stories and said witty things and sung songs until they were hoarse. The additions to their larder which George had been able to supply gave them a better supper than they were accustomed to, and they were merry over it.

None of the members of Bob's squad had ever seen the new scout before, and, although they treated him with the greatest respect, they were sadly disappointed in him. The scouts with whom they were familiar were great, rough, bearded men, strong of limb and slovenly in dress, who had lived among the Indians all their lives, and had the reputation of being able to whip their weight in wild-cats; but this one looked as though he had but just come out of a fashionable tailor's shop, and, moreover, he was nothing but a boy in years. What could the colonel have been thinking of when he engaged this stripling to lead men across the river and into the midst of the desperadoes who were known to have their strongholds there? It was dangerous work, and the guide ought to be a person of courage and experience; and George didn't look as though he had either. That was what the troopers thought as they sat at the table casting furtive glances at the new scout, who was talking earnestly with Gus Robbins; but it was not long before they found out that it took a brave man to follow where he dared lead.

The first trooper who finished his supper took the place of the sentry at the door, and the next relieved the one who was standing guard over the dug-out. When these two had satisfied their appetites the dishes were washed, the table was laid again and the deserters were ordered up. Some of them appeared to be very much disheartened, and would scarcely look their comrades in the face, while the others were so defiant, and had so much to say about the colonel who had ordered their arrest and the men who had carried those orders into execution, that Bob was obliged to warn them that if they did not eat more and jaw less he would put them back into the dug-out without any supper.

When the deserters had had all they wanted to eat they were sent down to their prison, the outside sentry was relieved, and Bob stood guard at the door, with George for company. They had much to talk about, and it was long after midnight when they went to bed. They slept on the same blankets, and the new scout went off into the land of dreams with his arm thrown lovingly around the boy who had twice saved his life, and whom he had never expected to see again.

CHAPTER VI

AN UNEXPECTED GUEST

"Well, old fellow, what do you think of me now?"

It was George Ackerman who uttered these words, and the question was addressed to his herdsman, Zeke. The former stood in front of a full-length mirror that hung against the wall (among other extravagant and useless things for which Uncle John had spent his nephew's money were two elegant pier-glasses, one for his own room and the other for Ned's), and Zeke was sitting on the edge of a chair, with his elbows resting on his knees and his chin supported by his hands.

When the commander of Fort Lamoine accepted his proffered services, George had asked for and received a furlough for thirty days to enable him to procure an outfit and to consult with his guardian in regard to the management of the ranche during his absence. That furlough had nearly expired, and George was about to start for the fort. The honest fellows who had so long been employed on the ranche that they began to look upon themselves as members of the Ackerman family could not bear the thought of parting from him, and Zeke especially felt very gloomy over it. He had often denounced, in the strongest terms, the circumstances which seemed to render it necessary that his young friend should cast his lot among the soldiers for a season, and on this particular morning he looked as though he had lost everything that was worth living for.

George had just put on his new uniform for the first time, and no one, except a very intimate acquaintance, would have recognized in him the rough-looking cowboy whom we introduced to the reader in the first volume of this series of books. During the eighteen months he had lived in the pilot-house he had fallen in with some of the ways of those by whom he was surrounded, and grown very particular in regard to his personal appearance, although he did not by any means go to extremes, as his cousin Ned had done. As he placed the jaunty fatigue-cap over his long, curly hair he looked rather complacently at the handsome face and figure that were reflected from the polished surface of the mirror.

"Come, Zeke, don't be cross," said he, walking up to his herdsman and giving him a slap on the back. "Say just one kind word to me before I go."

"I won't," growled Zeke in reply.

"Then wish me good luck in my new calling," added George.

"I won't," repeated the herdsman in a still louder tone. "You're always going off on some new callin' or another, an' I don't see no sort of sense in it. Didn't I stay home here, quiet an' peaceable, takin' care of your critters, while you was a-philanderin' up and down the river on boats that was likely at any minute to burn up or bust their boilers? Now that you have got safe home again, why in creation don't you stay here? Good land o' Goshen!" shouted Zeke, jumping up, spreading out his feet and flourishing both his huge fists in the air, "of all the fool notions that ever a livin' boy got into his head—"

"That'll do, Zeke," interrupted George with a laugh. "I have heard that a thousand times, more or less, already. You will bid me good-bye when I get ready to go, I suppose?"

"I s'pose I won't do nothin' of the kind," exclaimed Zeke. "Of all the fool notions that ever a livin' boy—"

"I understand. Come here and pack my clothes-bag for me; you can do it better than I can."

"I won't. Them things is goin' to hang you higher'n the moon the first you know," said Zeke, scowling savagely at the elegant Mexican costume which George lifted from the bed. "Don't you never go 'crost the river with them duds on, 'cause if you do Fletcher'll string you up for a spy."

"Not in peace-times, I guess," answered George.

"What odds does it make to sich as him whether it's peace-times or not? You'll see."

"Well, he will have to catch me before he hangs me. Go and tell the cook that I am getting tired of waiting for breakfast."

"I won't; I won't never do nothin' for you no more, nor say another word to you, nuther."

"I am sorry you feel so bad about it," said George as he proceeded to pack his clothes away in a canvas bag he had provided for that purpose; "but the thing is done, and it can't be undone."

"I don't care if the Greasers come over here next full moon an' steal every huf an' horn you've got," exclaimed the angry herdsman.

"I do," replied George; "I don't want them to do anything of the kind. I don't want them to steal another steer from me or anybody else, and that is the very reason I became a scout. Our troops are going to teach those fellows to stay on their own side of the river, and I am going to help them do it."

"There's enough without you," growled Zeke.

"Suppose that everybody thought so; where would we get the men to fight our battles?—What in the world is that?"

For just then there was a terrific uproar on the porch. Above the stamping of heavy boots and hoarse but subdued ejaculations of rage, such as men sometimes utter when they are engaged in a fierce struggle, arose the voice of one who spoke in pleading accents, but whose words suddenly ceased with a kind of gasping sound, as if his throat had been seized by a strong hand. Zeke sat up on his chair and looked at George, whose face expressed the utmost bewilderment. Before either of them could speak the door was thrown open with great violence, and a dishevelled and half-strangled man, dressed in a dingy blue jacket and a pair of dirty leather trousers, was pitched into the room, with such force that when he brought up against Zeke that worthy herdsman was knocked out of his chair, and the two came to the floor together.

"What do you mean by such work as this?" demanded George, looking first at the prostrate man and then toward the door, where stood Jake and Bob with their hands clenched and their faces flushed with anger.

"Jest take a good squint at that feller's figger-head an' answer the question for yourself, Mr. George," answered Jake, shaking his fist at the man who had been so unceremoniously introduced into the room.—"Give it to him good an' strong,

Zeke!—Well! I'll—be—blessed!—Won't you, Bob?"

This exclamation was called forth by an action on the part of George Ackerman that astonished Jake and Bob beyond measure. Zeke had instantly recognized the man who had so unexpectedly prostrated him, and, seizing him by the back of the neck in his iron grasp, began shaking him as a dog would shake a rat. George also recognized the man after he had taken a second look at him, and springing forward he seized Zeke's arm and tore his grasp loose. Then he assisted the man to his feet, and taking his hand in his own shook it cordially.

"Well, I *will* be blessed!" repeated Jake, who stood looking the very picture of astonishment.—"Won't you, Bob?"

"I should say I would," replied the latter, who was equally amazed. "That's something *I* never expected to see—an Ackerman shaking hands with a cattle-thief!"

"Springer," exclaimed George, "I am glad to see you again; and without your crutches, too! I hope you have entirely recovered."

Yes, the man who had made his entrance into George's room in so unusual a manner was Springer, whom we have often spoken of as the wounded cattle-thief. He had, as we know, once been in the employ of George's father; but proving to be utterly unfit for the position he held, Mr. Ackerman had discharged him, and Springer had sought revenge by making an unsuccessful effort to burn the ranche. Of course he could not stay in Texas after that, so he fled across the river and joined his fortunes with the Contra-Guerrillas, a regiment of desperadoes in the employ of the ill-starred Maximilian. He belonged, with other renegade Americans, to Fletcher's band, who were the principal foragers for Maximilian's army; but instead of robbing the adherents of Juarez, who probably had no stock worth stealing, they made numerous raids across the river and ran off the cattle belonging to the Texans. Springer was one of the band who stampeded George's herd at Catfish Falls, and during the short skirmish that followed Zeke sent a bullet through each of his legs, wounding him severely. He managed to keep up with the band a few miles, but the rapid motion was too much for him, and he was finally abandoned by his companions, who hurried the captured cattle toward the river, leaving Springer to look out for himself.

The pain occasioned by the wounds that had been inflicted upon him by Zeke's Winchester was so intense that the raider was forced to travel very slowly. Arriving on the banks of a little stream that ran across the trail he was pursuing, he rolled out of his saddle to quench his thirst, which had became almost unbearable; but his bridle slipping from his hand, his horse wandered away, and, as Springer was not able to walk, he could not catch him again. He sank helplessly down beside a tree, where he was presently discovered by George Ackerman, who was making his way on foot toward Mr. Gilbert's ranche. The boy ministered to his wants by bringing him water in his hat and sharing with him his slender stock of provisions, and Springer showed his gratitude by warning George of a plot which his uncle John and cousin Ned had laid against him. He went into all the details, but George refused to believe a word of it until subsequent events, which we have already described, proved to his entire satisfaction that the thief had told him nothing but the truth.

After spending half an hour in the man's company, George caught his horse, assisted him into the saddle, and Springer succeeded in crossing into Mexico without being discovered by any of the settlers whom Zeke had gathered together to recapture George's herd. He made his way to Don Miguel's ranche, and there our hero found him when he was captured by Fletcher's men. The raider seemed to be sorry for his misdeeds, and George had assured him that if he ever made up his mind to turn over a new leaf and lead a different sort of life, he would assist him by every means in his power.

"Springer," said George, drawing up an easy-chair for the use of his guest, "what brought you over on this side of the river? Have you abandoned Fletcher for good?"

The cattle-thief gasped and coughed three or four times, as if he were trying to clear his throat of something that stuck there and choked his utterance, and finally nodded his head in reply.

"Don't pay no attention to him, Mr. George!" exclaimed Bob. "He don't know nothin' but stealin' an' lyin', that feller don't, an' I wouldn't trust him as far as I could sling a yearlin'."

"If it wasn't for sich fellers as him you could stay to hum quiet an' peaceable like, an' not have to go off fur a soldier," added Jake.

"When I was a prisoner among the Greasers he gave me advice that assisted me in making my escape, and why should I not treat him kindly?" demanded George, turning indignantly upon the speakers. "No visitor at the Ackerman ranche was ever treated so shamefully before, and I tell you I don't want the thing repeated."

"Why, Mr. George," stammered Jake, "he rid up to the porch an' said he wanted to speak to you, an' so we brung him in— me an' Bob did."

"Go and tell the cook to put another plate on the table and to hurry up breakfast," said George with an air of disgust.

"Mr. George," said Zeke solemnly, "do you mean by that that you're goin' to break bread with this—this varmint?"

"I mean that Springer is going to eat a good breakfast with me, if that is what you want to know," replied George.

"Then, Bob, you needn't say nothin' about that there other plate," continued the herdsman, picking up his hat and moving toward the door. "Springer can have the one I was goin' to use."

"Zeke, sit down and behave yourself," exclaimed George.

"No, I won't. I ain't agoin' to eat salt with a man what tried to burn this ranche over your dead father's head, an' you a little babby at the time, without no power to help yourself. I don't know what this family is comin' to, anyhow."

"No more do I," chimed in Bob, while he and Jake looked daggers at their employer's new guest. "Things ain't as they used to be in the good ole days. I won't wait on no table that he sets at."

As if moved by a common impulse, the three men left the room, Zeke closing the door behind him with no gentle hand. The cattle-thief seemed to be greatly relieved to see them go, but their extraordinary conduct made him very uneasy, and he looked toward George to see what the latter thought about it.

"Never mind them," said the boy encouragingly. "They were employed on this ranche before I was born, and have finally come to think that they have more rights here than I have. Now, what did you want to see me for? How can I help you? If I were going to stay at home, so that I could stand between you and the settlers, I would give you a herdsman's berth, if that is what you want; but I am going to Fort Lamoine as soon as I have packed my things and disposed of my breakfast, and I may not be back for a year. I am a United States scout."

"I wondered what you were doin' with them soldier-clothes on; an' that explains it," said Springer, speaking with difficulty. "I don't reckon you can help me none jest now, but mebbe I can help you by puttin' you on your guard agin' Fletcher."

"Is he after me again?" cried George. "I was in hope I had seen and heard the last of him."

"Them kind of fellers is always turnin' up when they isn't wanted," replied Springer. "He's come back to his ole hole at that there ranche, bringin' a good many of his ole men with him, an' some new ones that would be wusser than he is, only that ain't possible. Amongst them all, they have laid a plan to visit you next full moon."

"Let them come," said George, snapping his fingers in the air; "they'll not get me, or any stock either."

"He wants you more'n he wants stock," continued Springer. "That is, he wants you first. Your uncle John put the very mischief into that there feller's head, an' he's goin' to make a pris'ner of you, like he did afore. He knows that you are master here now—that you've got more money an' cattle than you know what to do with; an' he thinks you would rather give 'em all up than lose your liberty."

"No doubt I would," answered George, "but before he can make any demands upon me he must catch me. That he will never do, for the next time—"

He was about to say that the next time he saw Don Miguel's

ranche he would be so strongly backed up that he would stand in no fear of the boss cattle-thief and his band. But he didn't say it, for he did not know how far it would be safe to trust his friend Springer. He need not have been so particular on this point, however, for the cattle-thief knew as much about the contemplated movements of General Ord's forces as George did himself. The Mexican authorities had been notified that if the raids from their side of the river were not stopped our troops would take the matter in hand and punish the thieves wherever they could be found; and those same authorities had been accommodating enough to warn Fletcher, and so put him on his guard.

"Where have you been since I last saw you?" inquired George, "and what has become of my horse? What did the 'boss' say when he found I had slipped through his fingers? I told you I shouldn't stay there and allow myself to be robbed. Did he follow me?"

"No, he didn't foller you, 'cause nobody knowed till mornin' come that you had skipped out," answered Springer. "When Fletcher went to call you to breakfast, an' you wasn't there, he thought you was a-loafin' around somewheres about the ranche; but when somebody told him that the hoss with the four white feet, that follered us acrost the river on the night we tried to get the strong-box out of this house, was gone, he knowed in a minute what was up, an' he was about the maddest man you ever see. But he couldn't take time to hunt you up, an' all he could do was to swear that he'd hold fast to you the next time he got his hands on to you."

"He'll never get his hands on me again," said George confidently.

"I hope he won't, but if he does it'll be worse for you. That there black hoss of your'n is dead," continued Springer; "he was shot at Queretaro. You see, when we got down to the place where the fightin' was goin' on, we knowed in a minute that Max couldn't hold out much longer, so we started one dark night to cross over to Juarez. His soldiers seen us comin', an', thinkin' that we were up to some trick or another, they turned loose on us an' cut us up fearful."

"It served you just right," said George, with honest indignation. "You had no business to go in with Maximilian in the first place, but having joined him you ought to have stood by him to the last."

"We *did* stand by him after that, 'cause we had to," answered Springer. "But it didn't take 'em long to captur' the place, an' it didn't take them long either to say what should be done with Max. He an' Mejia an' Miramon were took out on a hill near the ruins of an old stone fort an' shot. I didn't see it, 'cause I was under guard with Fletcher an' the rest; but I heared some of 'em who did see it say that just before the shooting was done Max he says to Miramon, 'The bravest man should have the post of honor;' so he puts Miramon in the middle, an' Max he stood on the left. It was a mean piece of business all the way through," said Springer, drawing his hand nervously across his forehead, "an' I am powerful glad that I am well out of it. Now, Mr. George, seein' as how you belong to the army, mebbe I had oughter tell you something. You remember them two Greasers who shot that cowboy down to Rio Grande City, an' was put in jail for it, don't you? Well, they belong to our gang, an' Fletcher an' the rest are getting ready to go down there an' take 'em out."

"Very well. Go right down to the commanding officer at Eagle Pass and tell him of it," said George promptly. "Then come up to Fort Lamoine, and we'll see if the colonel won't do something for Fletcher when he comes over here to capture me."

"An' there's another thing I had oughter tell you, Mr. George," continued Springer, sinking his voice almost to a whisper. "I come over here as a sort of spy, like. I am to find out all I can about your ways—where you go of nights, an' all that, you know—an' then I am to go down to Rio City, take a look about the jail, see how many guards there are, an' everything else that is worth knowin', an' after that I am to go back an' tell Fletcher."

"I am glad you didn't say so while my men were in here," observed George.

"I was just a trifle too sharp for that," said Springer, shaking his head and looking very wise. "I don't want to make them any madder at me than they be now."

"But you are not going back to Fletcher with any news, are you? You told me you had left him for good."

"Mr. George," said Springer earnestly, "I ain't agoin' to take no news acrost the river that will do anybody there any good. I ain't forgot that you helped me when I was a-starving for grub an' water, and I ain't likely to forget it, nuther. I did say I had quit them fellers for good, an' when I said it I meant it; but you can see by the way your own men used me, right here under your nose, that I couldn't stay here without nobody to back me up. I can't starve, so I'll have to go back till you come home again."

"If you will stay on this side of the river I will see that you don't starve," replied George. "After you have told the commanding officer at Eagle Pass of the attempt that is to be made to release those murderers, come up to Fort Lamoine and I will find some honest work for you to do. The soldiers at the post are not acquainted with you, and consequently there will be no one to trouble you. I will say that you used

Harry Castlemon

to work for my father, and that will help you to a position."

While Springer was trying to make the boy understand how grateful he was to him for his kindness, there was a rap at the door, and Bob thrust his head into the room to announce in a surly tone that breakfast was ready.

"Where's Zeke?" asked George.

"Gone," was the laconic reply.

"All right! If he is foolish enough to go off without any breakfast, let him go. He'll meet me somewhere along the trail and say good-bye, I know. Bob," added George, pointing to the clothes-bag, which he had packed while he and his visitor were conversing, "put this into the pack-saddle, and have everything ready, so that I can start as soon as I have eaten breakfast.—Come on, Springer."

George led the way into an adjoining room, and found an excellent breakfast waiting for him. The cook, knowing that this was the last meal the young master of the ranche would eat at that table for long months to come, had exhausted all his knowledge of the cuisine in the effort to serve up a breakfast that would tempt George to eat, no matter whether he was hungry or not.

True to his promise, Bob kept out of the breakfast-room, and George and his guest were obliged to wait on themselves; but as they were used to that, they got on very well. While they were eating George once more repeated the instructions he had given Springer, and reiterated his promise to furnish him with steady employment and give him a chance to make an honest living.

Breakfast over, George accompanied his guest to the door,

and saw him ride away toward Eagle Pass. As soon as he was out of sight the boy went into the house after his weapons and to take leave of the servants, who were good-natured enough now that Springer was gone. After shaking them all by the hand, and listening to their hearty wishes for his safe and speedy return, he mounted his horse, which stood at the porch saddled and bridled, took his pack-mule by the halter and rode away toward Mr. Gilbert's ranche. The first person to greet him as he drew rein in front of the door was Zeke, who had so emphatically declared that he would not have another word to say to him.

"Where's that pizen varmint?" demanded the herdsman in no very amiable tones.

"Look here, Zeke," replied George, "if you should happen to meet that man while I am gone, I want you to treat him civilly; do you understand? If you see him in trouble, I want you to help him out. He is sorry for what he has done, and intends to lead a better life; and if you don't assist him in every way you can, you are not the fellow I take you for."

"Humph!" exclaimed Zeke contemptuously. "Sorry, ain't he? Wants to lead a better life, don't he? Well, it's mighty little chance he'll have if he makes a business of bumpin' up agin me the way he did this mornin', I bet you."

"He couldn't help it; Jake and Bob threw him against you. I know he is in earnest, for he has proved it. He came to the ranch to tell me that my old friend Fletcher is coming over to capture me next full moon, and he has now gone down to warn the officer in command at Eagle Pass that an attempt will soon be made to liberate the murderers who are in jail there.—Good-morning, Mr. Gilbert. I have stopped to say good-bye."

"Why don't you slap your foot down an' tell him he sha'n't go, Gilbert?" demanded Zeke.

"I am as sorry to have him go as you are," replied Mr. Gilbert. "But it is to our interest to do all we can to break up this raiding business, and George can do more than any of us. In fact, he is the only one in the settlement who can do anything, for you know the colonel wouldn't accept the services of our company of Rangers when we offered them to him.—Come in, George, and say good-bye to Mrs. Gilbert and the girls."

This was soon done, for the boy did not like to linger over the parting; but still, it was much harder for him to take leave of these good friends than he thought it would be. The whole family accompanied him to the door, and when he came out Zeke turned his back to him.

"Say good-bye to me," said George, giving him a pat on the shoulder; "it's your last chance."

"I don't care if it is," shouted the old fellow; "I won't do it."

"Then I will say it to you: Good-bye, Zeke. It will be a long time before I see you again, if indeed I ever do, but I never shall forget you. You have been a good friend to me."

This was altogether too much for the honest herdsman. He faced quickly about, and, seizing George's hand with a grip that brought tears to his eyes, churned it up and down like a pump-handle. Then he dropped it and turned away, while George, without saying another word, vaulted into his saddle and rode off. Zeke watched him as long as he remained in sight, and then in broken accents addressed the silent group who stood in the doorway:

"Thar's that there boy."—here he waved his hand in the direction in which George had disappeared—"he was all I had, an' now he's gone off to fight them Greasers without askin' me would I let him go. I toted him in them there arms when he was a yellin' babby not knee-high to a duck; I put him on the fust hoss he ever rid; I slept under the same blanket an' herded cattle with him when he got bigger; I larnt him how to throw the lasso an' shoot the rifle; an' now he's went off an' left me alone! Dog-gone them pizen Greasers!" roared Zeke, flourishing both his fists in the air.

He lingered a moment, looking rather sharply at Mr. Gilbert, as if he had half a mind to take him to task for giving his consent to George's "fool notion," and then, thinking better of it, he lumbered down the steps, mounted his horse and galloped off toward the place where he had left his herd in charge of an assistant.

George camped two nights on the prairie, and on the third afternoon, an hour or two before sunset, he arrived within sight of one of the stage-company's deserted stables. Or, rather, it *was* deserted the last time he saw it, but now there was an armed soldier in front of the door, and he was presently joined by others, one of whom, by signs, invited him to approach. George complied, and presently found himself surrounded by a squad of troopers under the command of Corporal Bob Owens, who greeted him as we have described.

CHAPTER VII

HOW BRYANT WAS CAPTURED

Reveille was sounded the next morning by Corporal Owens, who, having no drum or bugle at his command, sprang up at daylight and aroused his slumbering companions by shouting out the order, "Catch up!" More from the force of habit than anything else, he called the roll while he was bundling up the blankets on which he and George had slept, and, making the sergeant's salute to an imaginary officer, he announced: "All present or accounted for." Then Carey was ordered to boil the coffee, and Bob and the three troopers who were off duty went out to groom the horses. Having brought no brushes or currycombs with them, they were obliged to content themselves with rubbing the animals down with handfuls of grass; but they "went through the motions," as Bob expressed it, and that was all the most exacting officer could have expected of them under the circumstances.

As soon as breakfast had been eaten the troopers and their prisoners set out on the return march, Bob and the new scout leading the way. Behind them came the deserters, guarded on each flank and in the rear by two cavalrymen. Their advance was necessarily slow, for the captives had travelled rapidly the day before in order to put a safe distance between themselves and the fort, and they were weary and footsore.

Gus Robbins, especially, was nearly "done up." He was in a worse condition than Talbot was, for the latter seemed to have slept off the effects of his wound. George felt the greatest compassion for Gus, and offered to lend him his horse; but Bob, who had grown somewhat hardened to suffering during his experience in the army, positively forbade it.

"It wouldn't do, George," said he, looking admiringly at his friend's sleek, well-conditioned animal, which was constantly champing his bit and tossing his head as if he were growing impatient at the slow progress they were making. "Gus would make a break for liberty sure, and as that nag of yours is able to distance anything in my party, I'd have to—" Here Bob tapped his carbine significantly. "That's something I don't want to do. Gus isn't so nearly exhausted as he seems to be. He is more distressed in mind than he is in body, for he is thinking of the prison at Fort Leavenworth. After we have gone a few miles we will rest them by taking them up behind us, but it wouldn't be a very bright trick to give one of them a horse to himself."

About eleven o'clock a halt was ordered, and the deserters, who were riding behind the troopers, having dismounted, Corporal Owens took Carey off on one side and gave him some very emphatic instructions. Then he and George also dismounted, and, leaving their horses behind, made their way cautiously toward a ridge a short distance in advance of them. As they neared the top they threw themselves on their hands and knees and crept up until they could look over it. They were in plain view of the squatter's cabin at which the troopers had stopped to eat their dinner the day before. Bob took just one look at it, and then hastily backed down the ridge again.

"Did you see that fellow chopping wood in front of the

Harry Castlemon

shanty?" said he, addressing himself to George. "That's the man I am looking for."

"Are you sure?"

"Am I sure that I have a pair of good eyes?" asked Bob in reply. "Of course I am. I recognized him in spite of his citizen's clothes. That squatter has rigged him out in some of his own duds, but they'll not save him if I can manage in some way to get between him and the cabin."

"Perhaps, in order to make 'assurance doubly sure,' you had better take my field-glass and have another look at him," said George. "A false move might prove fatal to you, for it would show the squatter that you suspect him of harboring one of your men, and that would put both him and the deserter on their guard. But if that is your man, I am sorry for it."

"Why are you?" demanded Bob, looking at his companion in great surprise.

"I mean that I am sorry you found him here," George hastened to explain, "for the chances are that you will not take him without a fight. Peasley—that's the name of the owner of the cabin—is a notorious rough, and he would think no more of putting a bullet into you, if he thought he could escape the consequences, than he would of knocking over an antelope for breakfast."

"I thought he looked like that kind of a chap," said Bob. "Well, if he wants a fight he can be accommodated at very short notice. That's my man, and I am going to have him, squatter or no squatter."

As Bob gave utterance to this emphatic declaration he took the field-glass, which George handed over to him, crept up to the top of the ridge, and after taking a short survey of the cabin and its surroundings came back to his friend's side again.

"I knew I couldn't be mistaken," said he. "I had a fair view of his face, and as I have seen him every day for the last year, of course I couldn't fail to recognize him. The squatter is sitting on the porch smoking his pipe. Now, how shall I go to work to nab him? That's the question."

"Ride straight up to him and tell him that you want him," answered George. "I know of no easier way. I will go with you and see that Peasley doesn't double-team on you."

"But Bryant will run into the house the moment he sees me," said Bob.

"Then run right in after him and pull him out again," answered George promptly.

"I am almost afraid to do it. You see, the civil law is supposed to be supreme, and we soldiers have to mind what we are about, or else there'll be a big row raised about 'military despotism' and all that. I'd have to surround the house and keep him in there until I could send to the post and get authority from the colonel to go in after him. That is something I shouldn't like to do, for I have carried this thing through so far without help from anybody, and I want to complete the work myself. If I should ask for advice, the colonel would probably send a shoulder-strap down here to rob me of all the glory I have won," added Bob with a smile.

"Oh, you needn't laugh over it," exclaimed George. "You have covered yourself with glory. It isn't every fellow who would go down into a dug-out to capture six armed men after one of them had given positive proof that he was not afraid

Harry Castlemon

to shoot. That bullet-hole in your coat is a badge of honor. Now, I have just thought of something: I have brought with me a full suit of Mexican clothes, and also a saddle and bridle of the Mexican pattern. You are just about my size—"

"That's the very idea—nothing could be better," exclaimed Bob, as he arose to his feet and led the way toward the place where he had left his men. "It will disguise me completely, won't it? I can ride up and get between him and the house before he suspects anything, can't I? But how about the squatter?"

"I'll join you as soon as I see that you have corralled your man," replied George. "And you had better tell your followers to hold themselves in readiness to come up promptly when I signal to them from the top of the ridge."

The troopers awaited the boys' return with no little impatience, for the long consultation they had held on the ridge convinced them that their officer had discovered something on the other side of it. Bob gave them a wink and a nod, which instead of satisfying their curiosity only increased it, and then, to the surprise of all of them, began to divest himself of his outer clothing, while George threw off the canvas covering that protected his pack, and drew out of it an elegant silver-mounted saddle and bridle, and also a suit of clothes made in the height of the Mexican fashion.

"If that man of yours is at all sharp he will notice those army-brogans the first thing, and so you had better pull them off and put on these," said George, tossing a pair of light patent-leather shoes toward Bob. "There are the spurs. You had better take my horse too, for that 'U. S.' brand on your own nag would give you away in a minute. Now go easy, like an honest Greaser who is going about his legitimate business. Take my mule with you, for if you try to separate him from the horse he'll raise row enough to scare all the deserters out of the State."

It is wonderful what an alteration is sometimes made in one's appearance by a mere change of clothing. After Bob had got into the Mexican suit and exchanged his cap for the wide sombrero with its gaudy cord and tassel, it was doubtful if there was one among his brother-troopers who would have recognized him if he had chanced to meet him unexpectedly. Although he was not quite yellow enough for a Mexican, he was nevertheless pretty well tanned, and George assured him that all he needed was a black moustache and a long goatee to transform him into a very good-looking Greaser.

Everything being in readiness, Bob mounted George's horse, took the pack-mule's halter, which his friend passed up to him, and, after giving Carey instructions to bring up the squad and the prisoners promptly when he was signalled to do so, he rode slowly away, the new scout following a short distance in his rear, mounted on Bob's nag.

Arriving at the top of the ridge, Corporal Owens rode over it without pausing, and had not proceeded far before he became aware that he was discovered. The squatter got up and came to the end of the porch, the deserter ceased his chopping and leaned on his axe, and both shaded their eyes with their hands and looked at him. It was plain that they were not very well pleased with the result of their observations, for, after gazing at him for a few seconds, the squatter returned to his seat and puffed furiously at his pipe, and the deserter resumed his chopping. At the same moment the dogs appeared in force from under the cabin, their every action indicating that they had been summoned by the voice of their master. They looked up at him, wagging their tails vigorously, and then, encouraged, no doubt, by a low hiss or an order to "hunt 'em up," began running about with their

Harry Castlemon

heads high in the air. Discovering the approaching horseman, they started for him on the instant, each one striving to lead in the race and to growl and bark louder than his companions.

"They don't think much of Greasers in this part of the country," said Bob to himself; "and I don't blame them. If I were a stock-raiser I shouldn't feel very hospitably inclined toward a class of men who are always on the watch for a chance to jump down on me and steal my cattle. I wonder if I shall have pluck enough to dismount in the midst of all these dogs and make the arrest?" added Bob as the fierce brutes closed about him, all of them with their ears laid back close to their heads and their hair turned the wrong way, and some crouching at his side as if they were about to spring up and pull him out of his saddle.—"Get out! If you interfere with my business there won't be as many of you to-night as there were this morning. Aha! there's one of you out of the muss already."

For just here the mule gave a tug at his halter, and Bob, looking over his shoulder to see what was the matter, caught a momentary glimpse of a tawny body as it rose in the air, and, turning a complete somersault, landed on the ground all in a heap. One of the dogs, in his eagerness to do something grand, had approached a little too close to the mule's heels— an impertinence which that sagacious quadruped promptly resented by kicking out with both hind feet and knocking his would-be assailant into a cocked hat. The dog was not killed, but he was terribly demoralized, and his howls of anguish did much to dampen the ardor of his companions, who quickly withdrew to a more respectful distance.

Bob rode straight up to the house, but the squatter never looked at him, nor did the deserter stop his work. He drew rein in front of the porch, swung himself out of the saddle as quick as a flash, and, paying no attention to the dogs, which bayed him at a distance, but were too cowardly to assault him, he walked up to the deserter and tapped him on the shoulder.

"Bryant, I want you," said he.

The deserter, whose back was turned toward Bob, wheeled on the instant, revealing a face that was as white as a sheet. Bob backed around a little, so that he could keep one eye on Bryant while he watched the squatter with the other, and saw the man spring to his feet in the greatest astonishment, his pipe dropping from his mouth as he arose.

"You didn't expect to see me again so soon, did you?" said Bob, addressing himself to nobody in particular.

"Corporal Owens!" gasped the deserter, retreating a step or two, at the same time grasping his axe firmly in both hands and lifting it over his head. "Keep away from me; if you come a step nearer I'll—"

"Drop it!" commanded Bob sternly; and Bryant obeyed, for he saw the muzzle of a cocked revolver looking him squarely in the face.

All this happened in less time than we have taken to tell it, but meanwhile the squatter had not been idle. Quickly recovering from his amazement, he darted into the cabin, and just as Bryant dropped the threatening axe he appeared upon the porch with his rifle in his hand. Cocking it as he drew it to his face, he covered Bob's head with the weapon, and said, in a voice that trembled with rage and excitement,

"Look a here, young fellow, that's a game two can play at. Lower your shootin'-iron or I'll make daylight shine through you."

"Plump him over, Peasley!" cried Bryant, "plump him over! You are not going to stand there and let him take me back to the fort, are you? You promised to protect me. Plump him over! put the dogs on him! Do something, and be quick about it."

Bob bore himself with surprising courage during this trying ordeal. He did not know at what instant the squatter might comply with Bryant's frantic order to "plump him over" or to "put the dogs on him," but he never flinched. He did not even change color; and there is every reason to believe that his bold front saved his life.

"Bryant," said he in a calm voice, "don't you know that the colonel will be sure to hear of this, and that you are only making a bad matter worse by holding out against the inevitable?—As for you, Peasley, you've got the drop on me, and you can shoot if you feel like it; but if you do you are a gone squatter. Look there," he added, jerking his thumb over his shoulder.

Peasley looked, and saw George Ackerman coming down the ridge at a furious gallop.

"That is one of my backers, and there are six more who will be along in a minute. What did I tell you?" exclaimed Bob as the troopers and their prisoners came into view over the top of the ridge. "Now, Peasley, if you don't behave yourself I'll take you to the fort under arrest. I am in the discharge of my duty, and I am not going to put up with any more nonsense."

The squatter lowered his rifle, looked first at Bryant and then at the troopers, and seemed undecided how to act. While he hesitated George Ackerman dashed up to the porch, jumping out of his saddle before his horse had fairly stopped, and, knocking the dogs right and left with the heavy cavalry sabre which he had found fastened to Bob's saddle, he mounted the steps and laid hold of the squatter's rifle.

"Peasley, what are you about?" he exclaimed as he twisted the weapon out of the man's unresisting grasp. "Are you a born idiot? If you are not, don't you know that if you raise a fuss here you won't have any roof left over your head in less than five minutes?"

The squatter, muttering something under his breath, went back to his seat and picked up his pipe, and in a few minutes more the troopers and their prisoners arrived. At a sign from his officer, Loring dismounted and stood guard over Bryant, while Bob walked up to the porch.

"What do you think of the situation now, friend Peasley?" said he cheerfully. "I can't take that man to the fort in those clothes, and so I would thank you to trot out his uniform."

"Don't know nothing 'bout no uniform," growled the squatter; "ain't none here."

"I know better," answered Bob. "There is one here, and I must have it. You can either bring it out yourself or I shall search for it; and I give you fair warning that if I turn my boys loose in your shanty they'll handle things rough.—Now, what shall I do if that threat doesn't start him?" said Bob to himself. "I'll search the cabin and take the consequences; that's what I'll do."

"Come, Peasley, save yourself trouble by bringing out the uniform," said George. "There's no use in being a fool."

The squatter evidently began to think so too, for he sullenly rose from his seat and went into the cabin, coming out again in a few minutes with a bundle of clothing, which he threw spitefully down upon the porch. Bob quietly picked it up, and, carrying it down to Bryant, commanded him to pull off the squatter's clothes and put on his own; and Bryant at once complied, for he knew that if he did not Bob would detail two or three men to make the exchange for him. The new prisoner was then ordered to fall in with the rest, and the cavalcade once more took up its line of march for the fort; but a short stop was made as soon as they were out of sight of the squatter's cabin, during which Bob pulled off his disguise and put on his own garments.

"If I am ever obliged to wear this suit, I hope it will serve me as well as it has served you to-day," said George as he stowed the Mexican costume away in his pack and placed the silver-mounted saddle and bridle on top of it. "I didn't think it would so soon be brought into use."

"If it hadn't been for that same suit I might have got myself into trouble," said Bob. "Knowing where Bryant was, I never should have gone back to the fort without him, and if he had taken refuge in the house I might have gone in after him. What the colonel would have said to me if I had done that, I don't know."

During the ride to the fort Bob Owens, to quote from the troopers, "laughed all over." It was plain to everybody that he was highly elated over the results of the expedition, as he had an undoubted right to be. The pursuit and capture of the deserters had been conducted with considerable skill, and with as much determination as any veteran officer could have exhibited. Now that the danger was over, and his efforts to carry out the orders of his superior had been crowned with complete success, Bob was rather proud of that bullet-hole in his coat.

The next time the order was given for the troopers to take the prisoners on their horses, George beckoned to Gus Robbins, who quickly mounted behind him. After conversing a while upon the various exciting incidents that had transpired while Gus was Ned Ackerman's guest at George's ranche, the latter said,

"I never expected to meet you again, and I would rather not have met you at all than see you in this scrape."

"Well, it can't be helped now," answered Gus, with a weak unsuccessful attempt to appear defiant. "The colonel told me just what I might expect if I were ever again court-marshaled for desertion, and I went at it with my eyes open. I am not sorry I tried it, but I am sorry I didn't get away. If they don't watch me pretty closely, they will never have a chance to take me to Leavenworth."

"What do you suppose your father will say when he finds it out?" asked George.

"He will never find it out if I can help it."

"Don't you correspond with him?"

"Not by a great sight. He doesn't know whether I am dead or alive. I wish I had changed my name when I enlisted."

"He lives in Foxboro', Ohio, I believe?" said George.

Gus replied that he did.

"Is his name Gus too?"

"No; his name is Thomas, and he is—I say," exclaimed Gus suddenly, "what are you asking so many questions for? Do you intend to write to him about me?"

"Why, what object could I possibly have in doing that?" asked George, turning a very innocent-looking face toward the deserter. "I am sure it is none of my business what you do. Let's talk about something else. We are getting over the ground pretty rapidly now, and if Bob would let me I could land you in the fort in four hours. I don't suppose that you are in any hurry to get there, but what I meant was, that your additional weight would not prevent this horse of mine from travelling from here to the fort at his very best licks."

"No, I don't weigh much now," said Gus with a sigh. "Hard work, hard fare, hard treatment and constant worry have brought me down to a hundred and ten pounds."

"That's not very heavy for a seventeen-year-old boy."

"Oh, I am nineteen," said Gus, "but just now I feel as though I were forty."

"And you look so, too," said George to himself.—"That was the reason I wanted to know your exact age."

George had now learned all he cared to know about Gus Robbins. He was a minor, his father's name was Thomas and he lived in Foxboro', Ohio. He had gone to work in a roundabout way to gain this information, because he was afraid that if he asked Gus leading questions and told him what use he intended to make of his answers, the deserter would refuse to open his head. He had gained his point by strategy, and he did not intend that Gus should go to Leavenworth if he could help it.

Bob's supply of rations being nearly exhausted, his men and the deserters had a very scant dinner, and they did not get anything more to eat until they reached the fort. About ten o'clock that night they were challenged by one of the sentries, and, not knowing the countersign, were obliged to wait until the corporal of the guard was called. Having at last been admitted inside of the stockade, Bob marched up in front of head-quarters, where he ordered a halt, and he and George dismounted and went in to report to the colonel. Bob was very much astonished at the manner in which the officer greeted the new scout, and so was the orderly. They had never before seen him unbend to anybody as he did to George. Having never been admitted into head-quarters except when they had business there—some report to make, some orders to receive or some sharp reprimand to listen to—they knew the commandant only as a stern, exacting officer who seemed to care for nothing but the "regulations," and they had never imagined that he could be cordial or friendly with any one. But now they saw their mistake. The colonel got up from his seat, shook the boy warmly by the hand, told him he was glad to see him, called him by his Christian name and pointed him to an easy-chair, while Bob was left to stand at attention until the colonel got ready to attend to him.

"You are all ready for business I see, George," said the colonel as he resumed his seat at the table. "Well, I'll give you a taste of army-life by sending you out on a scout to-morrow. I will tell you about it pretty soon. There's your room," he added, pointing to an apartment adjoining his own, "and when you get ready you can bring in your luggage. The officer of the day will show you where to put your horse. You will have to be your own servant, unless you are willing to hire a civilian and pay him out of your own pocket. I saw that you came in with Corporal Owens: did he arrest you?"

"He was going to, sir," replied George, "but let me off when I showed him my furlough."

"Corporal," continued the colonel, turning to Bob, who stood lost in wonder, "what report have you to make?"

"I have the honor, sir, to report my entire success," was Bob's reply; "I've got them all."

"Where are they now?"

"On the parade, under guard, sir."

"Very good. Keep them there until further orders. Tell the officer of the day I want to see him."

George thought this was rather hard. Bob had risked his life and displayed most commendable zeal and ability in carrying out the colonel's orders, and now the latter dismissed him without one single word to indicate that he appreciated his services. Why did he not question the corporal in regard to the manner in which the capture of the deserters had been effected, and reward him for his gallantry by making him a sergeant on the spot? That was what George thought *he* would have done if he had been commandant of the post, and he then and there resolved that a full history of Bob's exploit should be laid before the colonel before he went to sleep that night.

CHAPTER VIII

GEORGE AT THE FORT

"Colonel, that young fellow has had a very hard time of it," said George when Bob had closed the door behind him.

"I expected it," replied the officer carelessly. "It is a wonder to me that the deserters didn't kill him, for there were some hard characters among them and they were well armed."

This remark would seem to indicate that the colonel was a most unfeeling man, and that he did not set much if any value upon the life of a non-commissioned officer; but such was not really the case. When he was a subaltern his superiors had often assigned to him some very hazardous undertakings, and when he attained to a rank that entitled him to a command he sent others into danger and thought nothing of it. A soldier's first and last duty was to obey any orders he might receive, and if he lost his life while in the act of executing those orders, why, it was nothing more than might be expected.

"They did try to kill him," said George. "Didn't you notice that hole in the breast of his coat?"

"I did, and I thought it looked as though it had been made by a bullet."

"So it was. Bristow shot at him. He wanted to be revenged on Bob for telling you about those thirty men who tried to desert some time ago, and if he had been a little better marksman you would have been put to the trouble of appointing a new corporal in the place of as brave a boy as ever swung a sabre."

"Why, George," exclaimed the colonel, becoming interested, "you are quite enthusiastic. Do you know Corporal Owens?"

"Yes, sir. He is the one who pulled me out of the river on the night the old Sam Kendall was burned."

"Oh yes; you told me about that the first time you were here. Where did the corporal find Bristow and his party?"

George answered this question by giving the colonel a circumstantial account of the pursuit, as he had heard it from Bob's lips, and the manner in which he had gone to work to secure the deserters after he had discovered their place of refuge. His description of Bryant's arrest amused the officer, who declared that it was a very neat piece of strategy.

Having placed Bob's case in the most favorable light possible, George then went on to tell the colonel about Springer's unexpected visit to his ranche, and described in detail the intended movements of Fletcher and his band. The officer said he had done right in sending the cattle-thief to warn the commandant at Eagle Pass, and had no doubt that that officer would take measures to assist the civil authorities at Rio Grande City in protecting the jail and giving Fletcher and his men a warm reception when they came across the river; but, in order to explain what happened afterward, we must here say that he did nothing of the kind. Unfortunately for Springer, he was recognized by some ranchemen who happened to be hanging about the post, and in spite of his protestations he was arrested and turned over to the marshal, who locked him up. No attention whatever was paid to his warning, and so positive was the marshal that there was "something back of it" that he would not even permit the prisoner to tell his story.

The cattle-thief remained in jail until the next full moon, and then Fletcher and his men suddenly made their appearance, just as Springer said they would. As no precautions had been taken to guard the prison, the raiders had an easy victory, and before assistance could arrive from the Pass, Springer and the murderers of the cowboy had been released and Fletcher was safe across the river. Springer, of course, was much too sharp to tell how he came to be an inmate of the jail, and the boss cattle-thief, believing that he had been arrested while trying to carry out his instructions, treated him with the greatest consideration.

"What did you mean by saying that you would give me a taste of army-life by sending me out on a scout to-morrow?" asked George after he had finished his story. "Any raiding going on about here?"

"Well, yes. I am going to send Clinton out to punish a war-party of Kiowas if he can catch them. I am aware you are used to roughing it, but you know nothing about campaigning with troops, and I thought I would give you a chance to get your hand in before I call upon you to lead us across the river. Some young bucks belonging to Satanta's band, the most of them mere boys, have broken away from their agency and come down here in pursuit of scalps and fame. Among other outrages which they have committed, they jumped down on a poor fellow the other day, killed or scattered his herdsmen, drove off his stock and carried his two children into captivity. I should like to be the means of ridding the frontier of that villain, for he is dangerous. During a peace-council that was held at Fort Dodge some time ago, Satanta talked so glibly about his desire to cultivate friendly relations with us, and his unalterable determination to 'follow the white man's road' in future, that he really succeeded in making the commissioners believe that he was sincere in what he said. To encourage him in his good resolutions, the department commander and staff presented him with a uniform coat and sash and a brigadier-general's hat. How the wily old scoundrel must have laughed in his sleeve when he saw how completely he had bamboozled some of our best soldiers!"

"How long did he keep his promise?" asked George.

"About three weeks, and then he led an attack, dressed in his new uniform, against the fort in which the council was held. Oh, he's a good one! I know you didn't come here to fight Indians, but you'll have to hold yourself in readiness for anything that turns up."

"You will always find me around when you want me," replied George. "May I write a letter here?" he continued, seeing that the colonel picked up his pen and turned to his table to resume some writing in which he had been interrupted when Bob and the new scout came in to report.

"Certainly. There are pens, ink and paper; help yourself. There's the letter-box over there. The mail-carrier goes out to-morrow."

Before George could begin work on his letter the officer of the day came in. He shook hands with the new-comer, to whom he had been introduced on the occasion of the boy's first visit to the fort, and was told by the colonel to put the deserters into the guard-house, to show George where to stake out his horse and mule, and to see that he had somebody to help him bring in his pack-saddle.

The work of bringing in his luggage and taking care of his animals was soon performed, and then George came back and began his letter. It took him a long time to write it, for he wanted to make it one that would produce an impression upon the person to whom it was addressed. It was to Gus Robbins's father. It conveyed to that gentleman the information that although his son was alive and in fair bodily health, he had brought himself into serious trouble, having been detected in two attempts at desertion, and unless his friends at home interested themselves in his behalf he had a fair prospect of going to prison. If Mr. Robbins would move in the matter he could easily procure the culprit's discharge from the service, for he was a minor and had enlisted without his father's consent; but if there was anything done it must be done quickly, for it was probable that a court-martial would be convened in a very few days. Having sealed and addressed the letter, he bade the colonel good-night and went to bed, feeling satisfied that he had done all he could for the unfortunate Gus.

George slept soundly, as he always did, but the morning gun and the first notes of reveille awoke him. While he was making his toilet with his usual care and deliberation—as we have said, his long intercourse with river-dandies had made him very particular on this point—his friend, Bob Owens, and the men who occupied the quarters with him, were hurrying on their clothes in order to get into line in time to answer to their names at roll-call. While they were dressing they talked, and this was a portion of the conversation that took place between the corporal and one of the colonel's orderlies—the same one who had been on duty when Bob went in to report his arrival with the deserters.

Harry Castlemon

"I say, Owens," exclaimed the orderly, "who was that nobby young officer who came in with you last night? What is his name, and what rank does he hold? I know he is green, for he didn't know enough to put on a dress-coat before he went into the colonel's presence."

"His name is George Ackerman," answered Bob, "but he is not an officer; he's a scout."

"'A scout'!" repeated the orderly in a tone of contempt. "He is a pretty-looking scout, I must say. What does he know about life on the Plains?"

"He knows a good deal more about it than anybody in this room, for he was born right here in Texas," was the reply.

"Has he ever seen service?"

"No, but he knows what danger is, and he has been in some situations that you wouldn't care to be placed in. During long months of his life he lived in constant fear of a violent death."

"I don't doubt that he told you so, but I don't believe it, all the same," observed the orderly.

"I can't help that. I am personally acquainted with him, and you are not. I was with him when the steamer to which he belonged was burned on the Mississippi River, and came to Texas with him. He owns a big cattle-ranche a few miles from here, and has an income of about forty thousand dollars a year."

"Aha! that accounts for the milk in the cocoa-nut," exclaimed the orderly. "I know now why it was that the colonel met him in so friendly a manner. Even those stern old regulars soften in the presence of one who was born with a silver spoon in his mouth, don't they?"

"But George Ackerman's money didn't get him the position he holds," said Bob quickly. "He has been a prisoner among the cattle-thieves on the other side of the river, and knows where they hang out. He is here to act as our guide when we pursue the raiders across the river."

"What did the cattle-thieves take him prisoner for?"

"Because they were promised twenty thousand dollars for it by George's guardian, who wanted to get him out of the way, so that his son could inherit George's property. But he managed to escape from them, went up North and became a pilot, and it was while he was serving in that capacity that I made his acquaintance."

"That's a very pretty story," remarked the orderly, "but doesn't it sound almost too much like a dime novel?"

"If you don't believe it ask Gus Robbins, if you get a chance to speak to him. He knows George, and has reason to be grateful to him too. Gus came down here to visit Ned Ackerman while the latter's father was acting as George's guardian, and got himself into trouble that would have ended seriously if George had not befriended him. It was through that same visit that Gus got into the army."

"Did you hear what the colonel said to him about a servant?" asked the orderly. "Whoever saw a scout with a servant? I never did, and neither did I ever before see a man holding that position treated with so much consideration by a post-commander. I can't account for it."

Bob could not account for it either, and so he attempted no

explanation. We may tell the reader that there were two good reasons for it. In the first place, George was not a regular scout; he might, with more propriety, have been called a volunteer aide. It is true that he was sworn into the service, and that he was bound to do his duty faithfully "during the pleasure of the commanding officer" of Fort Lamoine, but he drew no pay from the government. He did not even ask that he should be fed while he lived at the fort, but stood ready to pay his share of the mess-bill. He had freely offered his services as guide to the troops because he, in common with every rancheman and farmer in that country, wanted the raiding-parties broken up, and he believed that he could do as much, if not more, toward accomplishing that object than any other single civilian. He was not obliged to wear a uniform (being sworn in, he had a *right* to wear it), but he had purchased it for the same reason that he had purchased the Mexican costume and the other clothing he had brought with him—because he believed it might some day be of use to him. We have already seen how one of his disguises came into play. If he had not brought with him that Mexican suit, it is hard to tell how Bryant would have been captured.

In the next place, the colonel was an old acquaintance and friend of George's father. He had often enjoyed Mr. Ackerman's hospitality, and he could say, with Zeke, that he had carried George in his arms when the latter was a "yelling baby not knee-high to a duck," and when he himself was nothing but a second lieutenant. Since that time a great many things had happened. Mr. Ackerman and his wife were dead, the second lieutenant had passed through a terrible war, had worn a major-general's shoulder-straps in the volunteer army and won a brevet colonelcy in the regulars, and George had grown almost to manhood. Neither of them knew of the presence of the other in that country until George, accompanied by Mr. Gilbert and a few other ranchemen, came to the fort to offer his services. The colonel knew the boy as soon as he heard his name, and it was on account of the respect and affection he cherished for the memory of his father that he extended so cordial a greeting to him; but, like all the other soldiers who had seen him, the colonel did not think that George was just the guide he wanted.

"I need somebody with age and experience, George," said he, "and you have neither. I know you can handle a herd of cattle and manage your ranche in good style, but I am not so certain of your ability to act as guide to my troops. I admire your pluck, and I should be glad to have you come here and live until you get tired of it; and in order to make it lawful for you to stay here, I will give you a position as forage-master."

"I am very much obliged to you, sir, but that is a berth I don't want," answered George. "I want to help put down those raiders."

"But just think of the responsibility that would rest upon you," protested the colonel. "A single blunder on your part might cripple me fearfully."

"You need have no fears on that score," said Mr. Gilbert. "George is good wherever you put him. He is acquainted with Fletcher, who is the most active of all the raiders who trouble us; he knows where he hangs out, and he is the only one on this side of the river who does. When it comes to trailing, he is at home there too. Can you look at a trail and tell how old it is and how many men or horses made it?"

No, the colonel couldn't do that. He always looked to his scouts for information on those points.

"George can do it," said Mr. Gilbert. "He has served his time under one of the best trailers in the country; and that is Zeke,

Harry Castlemon

his herdsman."

After a little more conversation the colonel, although not without many misgivings, accepted the offer of George's services; and he never had occasion to regret it. During the very first expedition that was sent out of the fort after he reported there for duty he showed what he was made of, and gave the colonel reason for placing almost unlimited confidence in his judgment. Acting as Bob Owens's counsellor, he enabled the latter to perform an exploit that made him the lion of the post.

Having dressed himself, George passed through the colonel's office and out through the hall to the parade. In the outer door was seated a man who was bent half double, with his elbows resting on his knees and his face buried in his hands. Hearing the sound of the boy's footsteps, he raised his head, revealing a countenance so haggard and sorrowful that George was startled at the sight of it. The man moved aside to allow him room to pass, and then covered his face with his hands again, and as George walked out he was sure he heard him utter a suppressed moan. The man was not a soldier, for he was dressed in citizen's clothes. He looked like a rancheman; and as George was a rancheman himself, he naturally felt some sympathy for the unknown sufferer. After hesitating a moment, weighing in his mind the propriety of the step he was about to take, he turned back and asked,

"What is the matter with you, sir? Are you ill?"

"'Ill'?" repeated the man, without looking up. "Worse than that—worse than that."

"Is there anything that I can do for you?" asked George. "You seem to be in great trouble."

As these words fell upon his ear the man straightened up, and, gazing at George with a pair of wild-looking eyes, said, in a voice that was rendered husky by some strong emotion,

"I am in trouble, partner, and although I do not think you can help me in any way, I feel grateful to you for your sympathy. I have been bounced by the hostiles and cleaned out—completely cleaned out."

"That *is* bad," returned George, who told himself that the man took his loss very much to heart. He knew a good many stock-raisers who had been "bounced" and "cleaned out," but he had never before seen one who seemed to be so utterly broken down by his misfortunes as this one did. The stranger's next words, however, explained it all.

"The loss of my ranche and stock I don't mind," said he; "that's nothing. But when one sees his two motherless boys carried off by the red fiends, while he is powerless to help them, it's pretty rough, it's pretty rough."

"Why, this must be the man the colonel told me about last night," said George to himself.

"I should not fear that the savages would raise their hands against the lives of the boys (they are too young to be put to torture, one being eight and the other ten years of age) if it were not for one thing," continued the bereaved father, jumping to his feet and pacing back and forth like a caged tiger. "I made a hard fight of it, and dropped a Kiowa for every year of my oldest boy's age. Of course the death of those warriors will have to be avenged by their relatives. Perhaps you don't know it, but that is Indian law."

"I do know it," interrupted George. "I couldn't have lived so close to these raiders, both Indians and Mexicans, nearly all my life without learning something about their ways, could I? I am a Texan, like yourself."

"You are? I took you for a Yankee soldier."

"There's where you made a mistake," replied George. "I was born in Miller county in this State, and I am here to act as guide to the troops when they cross the river in pursuit of the cattle-thieves."

"Good! Put it there!" exclaimed the man, extending his hand, while his face for the moment showed the pleasure he felt at the meeting. "My name is Wentworth; what is yours?"

George told him, and Mr. Wentworth said he had often heard the name, and in a roundabout way had learned something of the family history.

"I have heard of you too," said George. "You have often been obliged to run in order to save your life and stock, have you not?"

"Yes, and I have always succeeded in getting safely away; but there is a first time for everybody, and mine came three days ago. I was going on to say that I am afraid the savages will take vengeance on my helpless little boys for the braves I shot in the fight," continued Mr. Wentworth. "If they don't do that, they will probably hold them for ransom; but they might as well tomahawk the boys at once and put them out of their misery, for I haven't a horn nor a hoof nor a cent of money to give in exchange for them. I know I have seen them for the last time, but won't I make it hot for those who stole them?"

George could not say anything comforting. The sight of the strong man's overwhelming grief struck him dumb.

"I know some of the bucks who were in the fight," continued Mr. Wentworth, grinding his teeth and rubbing his hands nervously together. "They have often camped on my ranche when they came down here buffalo-hunting. I don't care what treaties our government may make with that tribe; there will be eternal war between me and them. No Kiowa shall ever cross my trail and live—no, not if I hang for it. I only wish that some of those peace commissioners—those lunatics who believe that an Indian is a human being and needs only kind treatment to make him peaceable and friendly—could stand in my boots this minute. I tell you, Ackerman, if one of them were here now I'd stand and see an Indian shoot him, and never lift a hand in his defence. I got in last night and told the colonel about it, and he said he would send out a couple of companies this morning with orders to overtake and punish them if possible; but he might as well save his men and horses, for it isn't possible. They have reached the Staked Plains by this time, and are safe from pursuit. This is a lovely government for a white man to live under, isn't it? It is too cowardly to protect us from the Mexicans, and too tender-hearted to hang an Indian for murder unless he happens to kill some one high in authority, like General Canby."

Mr. Wentworth seemed almost beside himself when he thought of his boys, who were now so many miles away from him, for then it was that he realized how powerless he was to help them. He went on in this strain until he had talked himself out of breath, and then he went back to his seat on the doorstep and covered his face with his hands.

CHAPTER IX

WHAT GEORGE KNEW ABOUT TRAILING

"It is a hard case," said George to himself as he walked slowly toward the gate, "and I believe, as Mr. Wentworth does, that he has seen his children for the last time. In the first place, the chances are that the Indians, having so long a start, will not be overtaken; but if they go out of their way to attack other isolated ranches, and the troops should come up with them, their very first act, if they saw that they were likely to be whipped, would be to kill their captives, so that they could not be rescued. It *is* a hard case, that's a fact, and I don't see that anything can be done about it. I wish Zeke were here to give his opinion on the subject."

The troopers, having answered to the names, were going out to bring in their horses preparatory to grooming them, and George went with them to bring in his own. Nearly an hour was devoted to this important duty, which was performed under the watchful eye of an officer, and although George often saw his friend Bob, the latter did not speak to him. There were a good many shoulder-straps around, and work, and not talk, was the order of the day. Even those of the officers who, having no servants, were obliged to act as their own grooms, had very little to say to one another; but when these same officers were gathered around the breakfast-table half an hour later, they were lively and talkative enough. There they met on a footing of perfect equality, like the members of a private family, although the juniors did not forget to say "sir" when addressing their superiors. There were no orders issued during the progress of the meal, and in fact very little was said about military matters; but still, George heard enough to satisfy him that active operations against the thieving Kiowas were to be commenced immediately, and that he was to make one of an expedition upon whose success a good deal depended.

The appearance of the officers as they passed into the hall after rising from the breakfast-table must have been a signal to the bugler who stood in front of the door of head-quarters, for as soon as he saw them he raised his instrument to his lips and blew a shrill call. The clear, ringing notes had scarcely ceased when there was a commotion in the barracks, and a crowd of men came pouring out and hurried toward the stables. There were a hundred and twenty of them, and they belonged to the troops A, E and L—the latter commonly called the "Brindles"—of which Captain Clinton's scouting-party was to be composed.

"That's 'Boots and saddles,' George," said the colonel, who stood in the doorway appearing to notice nothing, but in reality keeping a close watch over the movements of the men to see that everything was done in accordance with the "regulations." "You are to go with Clinton, you know. Are you ready?"

"I will be in half a minute," replied the boy.

The stirring notes of the bugle, or the prospect of soon meeting face to face some of the bloodthirsty savages who had devastated Mr. Wentworth's home, must have excited George, so that he did not readily lay his hand upon the articles he wanted, for considerably more than half a minute elapsed before he again appeared with his Winchester on his back, a bag of cartridges slung over his shoulder and a revolver buckled about his waist. He ran to the stable, and had just put the saddle and bridle on his horse when another call of the bugle was heard. This was "To horse," and in obedience the troopers left the stable and fell into line on the parade, each man standing at the head of his nag. George did not belong in line—in fact, he did not know where he *did* belong—so he kept his eye on Captain Clinton, and when he saw that officer mount the horse which an orderly brought up to him, George at once placed himself in his own saddle, and, riding up to the steps where the colonel was standing, awaited further developments.

"Prepare to mount!" commanded Captain Clinton as he rode up in front of his own troop, and the words were immediately repeated by the other two company commanders.

In obedience to this order each trooper placed his left foot in the stirrup, and at the command "Mount!" which was given soon after, they all rose from the ground as if moved by the same set of springs, and seated themselves in the saddles at the same instant. No man was a half a second ahead or behind his companions. The three company officers then rode back to the colonel to report that their respective companies were ready to march, and after they had listened to some verbal instructions from him, they bade him and the rest of the officers good-bye, the bugle sounded the "Advance," and the troopers, moving four abreast—or, as a soldier would have expressed it, in column of fours—rode out of the gate. There they found Wentworth seated on a wiry little mustang, which looked altogether too small to carry so heavy a rider. Recognizing George, who rode by Captain Clinton's side, he gave him a friendly nod, and without saying a word turned his horse and rode away, the troopers following a short distance in his rear.

When soldiers are on the march and in no danger of immediate contact with the enemy, they are allowed numerous privileges, of which the troopers composing this particular scouting-party were not slow to avail themselves. Some of them drew their pipes from their pockets and filled up for a smoke, others threw one leg over the horns of their saddles and rode sideways, "woman-fashion," and conversation became general all along the line. But this talking and smoking did not interfere with their marching, for they rode rapidly, and made such good progress that by three o'clock in the afternoon they were within sight of the ruins of Mr. Wentworth's ranche. And a sorry sight it was, too. Nothing but a pile of blackened sun-dried bricks remained to mark the spot on which a few days ago had stood a happy home. Household furniture of every description was scattered around, but every article had been smashed beyond all hope of repair. What the savages had not been able to carry away with them they had ruthlessly destroyed. George did not wonder that Mr. Wentworth felt vindictive. The man did not have a word to say, but the expression that came to his face as he sat in his saddle gazing sorrowfully at the ruins of his home spoke volumes.

When the troopers came within sight of the ranche, George discovered that there was a horse staked out near the ruins, and that he had an owner in the person of a tall, gaunt man, who rose from the ground and rubbed his eyes as if he had just awakened from a sound sleep. His dress was an odd mixture of the civilized and savage. He wore a pair of infantryman's trousers, a rancheman's red shirt, and an Indian blanket of the same color was thrown over his shoulders. His head was covered by a Mexican sombrero, and his feet were protected by a pair of gaudily-ornamented moccasins. While waiting for the troopers to come up he filled a short black pipe and lighted it at the smoldering fire beside which he had been sleeping.

"That's Mountain Mose," said Captain Clinton in reply to George's inquiring look. "He no doubt gave himself the name because he has lived on the Plains all his life. He is a lazy, worthless vagabond, but what he doesn't know about Indians isn't worth knowing. If he would only wake up and display a little energy, he would be invaluable as a scout."

"What is he doing here?" asked George. "He seems to be waiting for us."

"Yes, I expected to find him at this place. He has been out to take a look at the trail of that war-party who did all this damage.—Well, Mose, any news?"

"Not much, cap," drawled the scout. "You put straight for the Staked Plains, an' if you are lively enough to ketch 'em anywhar, you'll ketch 'em thar."

"Then we shall never get the cattle," said the captain. "If the Indians are going in there, they intend that the stock shall die of thirst rather than fall into our hands."

"That's jest their little game, cap," said the scout, puffing at his pipe. "You see, they'll keep along on the edge of the desert, so't they can have grass an' water in plenty, an' if you don't pester 'em none they won't go into the Staked Plains at all; but if you push 'em hard they'll run the critters in thar an' leave 'em, hopin' that you will run your hosses an' men to death while you are huntin' 'em up. You won't never see the young ones, nuther; an' I don't see why the colonel sent out sich a party as this so late in the day, anyhow. We'd oughter been a hundred miles along that thar trail by sun-up this mornin'."

George felt the deepest sympathy for Mr. Wentworth, who listened attentively to what the scout had to say, although he said nothing in return. His almost overwhelming sorrow showed itself in his face, but did not take the form of words.

As Captain Clinton had made no halt for dinner, the colonel having instructed him to find and receive the report of the scout as soon as possible, he decided to stop here and allow his men an hour or two for rest and refreshment. Giving their horses into the charge of some of the troopers, he and his two company commanders walked away with the scout, while George rode off to hunt up Bob Owens. He staked his own horse out beside Bob's, and then walked back with him to take a nearer view of the ruins.

"How do you suppose that that man in the sombrero and moccasins knows that the Indians who did this have fled toward the Staked Plains?" asked Bob after he and his friend had spent some moments in silent contemplation of the savages' handiwork. "He certainly hasn't had time enough to follow the trail clear to those plains."

"Of course not," answered George. "But he probably followed it far enough to see that it leads in that direction."

"Well, explain another thing while you are about it," continued Bob. "I have been out on a scout before now after the hostiles, following a trail that was as plain as the nose on one's face, when all at once the scout would leave that trail and strike off over the prairie where there wasn't a sign of a pony-track."

"He was taking a short cut on the Indians," observed George.

"I know that, and sooner or later he would bring us back to that trail again; and sometimes we would have gained so much on the hostiles—who had perhaps been twenty-four hours' journey ahead of us when we left the trail—that we would find their camp-fires still smoking. Now, what I want to know is this: How did that scout know that those Indians were going to that particular spring or creek or ravine near which we found the trail?"

"Have you ever hunted foxes?" asked George.

"I should say I had. When I left home I owned a hound that couldn't be beaten in running them, for he was posted in all their tricks. But what have foxes to do with hostile Indians?"

"I am simply going to use the tricks of the one, which you understand, to explain the tricks of the other, which you do not understand," replied George. "They are a good deal alike in some respects. A fox, when he finds himself hard pressed, will resort to all sorts of manoeuvres to throw the hounds off the trail. One of his tricks is to run over a newly-ploughed field, if he can find one, where the scent will not lie. What would that brag hound of yours do in such a case? Would he waste valuable time in running about over that field trying to pick up a scent that wasn't there?"

"No, he wouldn't. He would run around the outside of the field until he found the place where the fox left it."

"Exactly. Now, an Indian is just as full of tricks as a fox is. When he is afraid of pursuit he will break his party up into small bands, and, although the trails made by these bands will lead in different directions at the start, you will find, if you break up your own party and follow them for a while, that they all tend toward the same points, where these little bands will all be reunited. Of course each of the trails will be obliterated as much as possible. Some of them will lead over rocky ground, where the hoof of a pony will leave no imprint; others will come to an abrupt termination on the bank of some stream; and others still will end at a place where the prairie has been burned over. When these war-parties break up in the way I have described, a place of meeting is always agreed on beforehand; and if a scout understands his business he can tell pretty nearly where that place is, for it is sure to be on the straightest and most direct route to the agency if the raiders belong to a 'friendly' tribe, or to their principal village if they belong to a tribe that is openly hostile. If these Kiowas take to the Staked Plains, they will probably enter it directly north of here, at its widest part. Then this Mountain Mose, if he is the scout he pretends to be, will leave their trail to take care of itself and draw a bee-line for the nearest water; and it will take thirty hours' rapid marching to reach it, too."

"How do you know? Have you ever been there?"

"No, but my herdsman Zeke has; and he has described the course to be followed so minutely that I can go there any day the sun shines or any night when the stars shine."

Bob did not say anything, but his friend noticed that he looked a little incredulous.

"It is not so difficult as it appears to be at first glance," George hastened to say. "Why, when a party of young Indians want to go into a strange country for plunder and scalps, they gather around some old warrior, who traces on the ground the direction in which they must travel in order to reach that country, describes all the water-courses and locates the principal landmarks to be found along the route; and with nothing but these verbal instructions to guide them, these little rascals, some of them not more than thirteen or fourteen years of age, will make a journey of hundreds of miles through a region that none of them have ever visited before. My bump of locality is not so large as an Indian's, but still I have a pretty good memory, and I have travelled many a mile through a strange country without going a step out of my way."

"What sort of a looking place is Staked Plains, anyhow?" asked Bob. "I have heard so many terrible stories told about it that I am almost afraid of it. What gave it that name? Are there any *stakes* there?"

Bob was inclined to be facetious when he said this, and consequently he was not a little astonished to hear George say in reply,

"There may not be any stakes there now, but there used to be. It *is* a terrible place, and many a wagon-train has left its bones there. It is big enough to get lost in, for it lacks only about six thousand square-miles of being as large as the State of New York; and although it is not exactly a desert, as we understand the word, it is a barren waste, where nothing living permanently resides on account of the great scarcity of water. A long time ago the Mexican traders marked out a route with stakes across the plain where they found a few small fountains, and that was what gave it the name it bears. Zeke says it is a perfect bake-oven. There are no trees to shelter you, no grass for your horses, no fuel to build a fire with, and an almost unearthly silence broods over it. I am not superstitious, but Zeke always speaks of it with a shudder, and I tell you I don't want to see any place that he is afraid of."

The two friends continued to talk in this way until Captain Clinton's cook came up and told George that dinner was ready. They rested half an hour after the meal was over, and then set out again, Mountain Mose leading the way and Mr. Wentworth, as before, riding by himself. As George was a sort of supernumerary, he was under little restraint, and consequently he rode where he pleased—sometimes in company with the scout, sometimes beside Captain Clinton, and then fell back to exchange a few ideas with Bob. He did not, however, waste much time with the scout. The latter was talkative enough until he learned that George held the same position that he did, and then he froze up at once.

"You're a pretty-looking scout, *you* be!" he exclaimed, moving his eye over the boy's trim figure. "Do you reckon you could tell the trail of a Kiowa from the track of a coyote?"

"Yes, I reckon I could," answered George with a smile. "But you need not be jealous of me, for I shall not interfere with you in any way. I came to the post to hunt Greasers, and not to trail Indians."

"Oh, you did, eh? So you're the chap that's goin' to show the boys the way acrost the Rio, be you?"

"I am," replied George.

"Well, all I've got to say is, that them that follers you is fools. I thought mebbe you was agoin' to poke your nose into my business; and that is something I won't put up with from nobody. If thar's anything I *do* understand, it's Indians."

This was true, but it sometimes happens that luck is not on the side of those who know the most. The scout would have given anything he possessed if he had been fortunate enough to perform the exploit that George assisted in performing before two days more had passed over his head.

Bob Owens did not fail to notice that there was not the least semblance of a trail to be seen anywhere. They had left it at the ruins of Mr. Wentworth's rancho, and he waited with no little impatience to see where they would pick it up again. He found out about sunset, for at that time the column reached the banks of a small water-course, and there they struck the trail, which was so broad and plain that it could be followed at a gallop. George, in company with some of the officers and the scout, spent a few minutes in looking it over, and then rode back to report the result of his observations to Bob Owens.

"There are not many warriors in the party," said he, "but they are so well supplied with horses that they can have a fresh mount every day if they want it."

"How do you know that?" asked Bob.

"Because I saw their tracks," replied George.

"That's not explicit enough. I suppose you did see the tracks of the horses, and so did I; but how in the world is a fellow going to tell whether or not those horses had riders on their backs? *That's* something that can't be done."

"Don't be too sure of that. Look here! Would you believe it if I should tell you that those Indians passed along here after daylight on Thursday morning?"

"No, I wouldn't," replied Bob bluntly. He could not, for the life of him, understand how anybody could draw such conclusions as these by simply looking at the print of a pony's hoofs in the grass; and if he had not been so well acquainted with George he would have inclined to the belief that his friend was "spreading it on" in order to make himself out a wonderful trailer. "I can't make head or tail of this business, and I don't believe you can, either; that is, I mean I don't see how you can."

"Well, listen while I explain," said George good-naturedly. "In the first place, I noticed, while we were passing through that belt of post-oaks back there, that some of the horses left a very devious trail, passing through thick bushes and under trees whose branches were so low that they would have swept a rider out of his saddle if he had not been on the alert to avoid them. Those horses were all loose."

"Perhaps not," exclaimed Bob. "The Indians might have passed through there when it was too dark to see where they were going."

"I know they might, but they didn't, as I shall presently show you. The horses which made those crooked trails were not mustangs. They were American horses, and their presence proves another thing that I didn't think to speak of before; and that is, that the Indians raided other ranches besides Mr. Wentworth's. How do I know that they were American horses? Because their tracks were larger than a pony's, and some of them were shod. The tracks made by the mustangs led through the open part of the timber, where there were no bushes and low branches; and this is one proof that the Indians did not pass through there in the night-time. If they had, they could not have kept in such open ground. I found further proof that these mustangs were all mounted by noticing that they did not stop to graze, as the loose horses did, being kept in constant motion by their riders. What do you think now?" asked George, seeing that Bob began to open his eyes.

"It reads like a book, don't it?" was Bob's reply. "But you have forgotten one very important thing. You said that the Indians passed through those post-oaks early on Thursday morning. How do you know that they didn't pass late on Thursday afternoon or early on Friday morning?"

"You think you have got me there, don't you? Well, you haven't. If there are 'sermons in stones and books in running brooks,' as the poet tells us there are, what is the reason that the print of an Indian pony's hoof may not contain a page of information that will prove to be useful to him who has the skill to read it? On Wednesday night there was a very heavy dew, if you remember."

"I don't remember," replied Bob; "I never pay any attention to such things."

"But you must pay attention to such things, and a good deal of it too, if you are going to be a Plainsman. During the last two nights there has been no dew at all. I noticed that some blades of grass, which had been pressed down by the hoofs of the horses and cattle, were covered with sand which stuck fast to them, having been dried on. This told me that the tracks were made while the grass was wet, and that the Indians had passed that way early on Thursday morning, or before the sun had risen high enough to dry off the dew. There were not more than fifteen or twenty of them. I didn't have time to see just how many, but they have stolen over a thousand head of steers and horses. Now, remember all I have told you, and see if I haven't made a pretty good guess."

"Do you think we shall catch them?" asked Bob.

"Well," answered George slowly, "raiding Indians *have* been overtaken and neatly whipped before now, but I have always believed that it was more by good luck than good management. These fellows will begin to show their tactics as soon as they find out that they are pursued. Then they will probably leave behind a few of the best mounted of the band to attract our attention and lead us away from the others, who will make all haste to take the prisoners and the stolon stock to a place of safety. If we bite at that bait, we shall lose everything, for as soon as the decoys have led us as far out of our way as they care to have us go, they will disappear all of a sudden, and we shall never see them again. If we keep on after the main body, and travel fast enough to gain on them, they will drop the stock in the desert, break up into squads of twos and threes, and we shall have nothing to do but to turn about and go home again."

The Indians did manoeuvre pretty nearly as George said they would, but Captain Clinton and his scouting-party did not go back to the fort until they had accomplished something.

CHAPTER X

HOW GEORGE SAVED THE CAMP

The troopers went into camp about midnight, having been nineteen hours in the saddle, during which time they had marched more than seventy miles. They halted on the bank of a small stream near a ford over which the Indians had passed during their retreat. The trail was plain, and some of the troopers, who did not know quite as much about trailing as they thought they did, declared that they were close upon the heels of the raiders.

"How is that, George?" asked Bob Owens, who had been detailed as one of the corporals of the guard. "Some of the boys say that if we should follow the Indians for an hour or two longer we would be within sight of their camp-fires."

"What makes them think so?" asked George.

"Because they have found tracks with the sand still running into them. Is that one of the signs by which to tell the age of a trail?"

"Under some circumstances, yes; in the present case, no. You could tell the age of a trail in that way if the ground around it had not been disturbed. This country about here is all quicksand, and you can take your stand almost anywhere along the banks of this stream, and by jumping up and down shake the ground for ten feet on all sides of you. When our heavy column crossed the ford and climbed this bank, it shook the earth, and that was what set the sand to running down into the tracks."

"I declare!" exclaimed Bob, gazing admiringly at his friend; "is there anything a trailer isn't obliged to know?"

"If he wants to be an expert he must keep his eyes and ears wide open, and pay strict attention to little things which almost anybody else would consider to be beneath his notice. It is wonderful what proficiency a person who has a talent for such things can acquire by practice. For example, this scout of ours could learn more about a trail in two minutes than I could in an hour. But he is fearfully jealous," added George with a laugh, "and you ought to have seen how mad I made him while we were passing through that belt of post-oaks this afternoon. Seeing that Captain Clinton was waiting very impatiently for information, I volunteered the statement that the hostiles had passed that way early on Thursday morning, and that Mr. Wentworth was not the only one who had suffered at their hands. The captain asked Mose what he thought of that, and Mose replied, 'I think jest this here, cap: if that kid is agoin' to lead this yere party he had better say so, an' I will go back to the post. He's a'most too fresh, an' he'd better go back in the woods an' practise at holdin' his chin.' But he did not contradict my statement, and that was all the evidence I needed to prove that I was right in what I said. The tracks here on the bank are not as fresh as you suppose. If they were wet, it would be a sign that the Indians crossed the ford since three o'clock this afternoon."

"Why since three o'clock?" asked Bob.

"Because the sun went under a cloud at that hour, and hasn't showed himself since to dry off the water that the horses and cattle brought out of the stream on their feet and legs."

While the two boys were talking in this way George was getting ready to go to bed. The camp was located at the foot of a perpendicular bluff which was perhaps twenty feet in height. On the top of this bluff the horses were picketed, and beyond them were the sentinels who were to look out for the safety of the animals and keep guard over their slumbering companions. Everything outside of the circle of light made by the camp-fires was concealed by the most intense darkness. Not even a star twinkled in the sky. George spread his blankets in a sheltered nook at the foot of the bluff and courted the "drowsy god" in vain. He was tired and his eyes were heavy, but he could not go to sleep. After rolling and tossing about for nearly two hours, he became too nervous to remain inactive any longer, so he slung his rifle on his back and climbed to the top of the bluff, where he found Bob Owens and two other non-commissioned officers sitting beside a fire and conversing in low tones. At another fire a short distance away sat Lieutenant Earle, the officer of the guard, nodding over his pipe.

"Hallo!" exclaimed Bob, "what brought you out here?"

"Oh, I want somebody to talk to," replied George, throwing himself on the ground by his friend's side, "Somehow, I can't sleep, and that's a new thing for me."

"You are not afraid of the hostiles, are you?" asked a corporal from the other side of the fire.

"Oh no, because I know that we have nothing to fear from them on such a night as this. If there were any hostiles in the neighborhood, they might slip up and steal a few horses, if they thought they could get away with their booty, but they wouldn't attack a party of the size of ours and bring on an open fight. It is too dark."

"Why, that is just the reason they *would* attack us," exclaimed the corporal, who, although he had often been on a scout, had never participated in a battle. "They rely upon the darkness to cover their movements and to assist them in effecting a surprise. I have read it a hundred times."

"Ah, yes," replied George—"story-book Indians make attacks at all hours of the day and night, but live Plains Indians don't. The reason for it is this: They believe that they will go into the happy hunting-grounds with just the same surroundings that attend their departure from this world. If an Indian is crippled or blind or ill, he will be just the same Indian in the spirit-land. If he dies from the effects of disease, he will suffer from that disease for ever; but if he is killed in battle on a pleasant day, and while he is in the possession of all his strength and faculties, he will go straight to the Indian's heaven under the most favorable circumstances."

"Suppose he is killed on a rainy day?" said the corporal on the other side of the fire.

"Or a snowy one?" chimed in a sergeant.

"Then he is doomed to paddle through rain or snow through all eternity," replied George; "and that he doesn't like either is proved by the fact that he will not stir out of camp while it is raining or snowing if he can help it. If an Indian is hanged, like Captain Jack or those thirty-seven warriors who were executed at Mankato in 1863 for participation in the Sioux massacre, he loses all chance of ever seeing the happy hunting-grounds. So he does if he is scalped; and that's the reason Indians make such efforts to carry off the body of a fallen comrade. A Plains Indian never willingly goes into a fight during the night. If he did, he would make it much warmer for us here on the frontier than he does now. He may make use of a night like this to get into position for an attack, but if left to himself he will not raise the war-whoop before daylight, because he believes that if he is killed during the dark he will be condemned to pass all eternity in darkness."

"Well, that is something I never knew before," said the corporal, "and I have been on the Plains a good many years. Now that I think of it—"

"Corporal of the guard, No. 7!" came the call through the dense darkness, whereupon Bob Owens jumped to his feet.

"What's the trouble out there, I wonder?" said he.

"Go and see," replied the sergeant with a sleepy yawn: "that's the only way to find out."

"Sergeant," said the officer of the guard, "if those horses have had grass enough, have them brought in and tied to the stable-lines. Look well to their fastenings."

"Corporal of the guard, No. 7!" came the call again; and this time it was uttered in a louder and more earnest tone.

Bob, who was walking toward post No. 7 with a very deliberate step, now broke into a run, and George jumped up and followed him. A fortunate thing it was for that camp and its inmates that he did so. His thorough acquaintance with the ways of some of the inhabitants of the Plains enabled him to prevent a catastrophe which would certainly have resulted in a serious loss of life, and brought Captain Clinton's scout to an inglorious end then and there. When he and the corporal reached post No. 7 they found the sentry on duty there lying flat on his stomach and gazing earnestly toward the horizon.

"What's the matter, Sprague?" demanded Bob.

"I don't know, I am sure," replied the sentry. "If the hostiles had made up their minds to pay us a visit, they wouldn't make such a racket as that, would they? There! don't you hear it? Something's coming this way, I tell you, and coming on a keen jump, too."

The three held their breath and listened intently. A second later the breeze brought to their ears the sound that had attracted the attention of the sentry—a deep, rumbling sound, faint and far off, but increasing perceptibly in volume. It resembled the constant muttering of distant thunder, but they all knew it was not that. Bob's face brightened at once, but George's grew pale. The corporal did not know the danger that threatened them, but his companion did; he had heard something like it before. He had heard it on the night that Fletcher and his band of raiders stampeded his stock, and he had thrown himself into an old buffalo-wallow and allowed three hundred frantic cattle to gallop over his head.

"Why, it must be cavalry from Fort Tyler," said Bob at length.—"But I'll tell you what's a fact, boys," he added, as a fresh gust of wind brought the sound more plainly to his ears: "there must be lots of them, for I never heard such a roar of hoofs before. They are coming this way, too. I hope they'll not run over us."

"Well, they *will* run over us," said George, speaking quickly but calmly, "unless you take immediate steps to prevent it. They are not cavalry; they are buffaloes."

"Oh! ah!" exclaimed Bob.

"Humph!" ejaculated the sentry, jumping to his feet.—"Don't tell the boys what I called you out for, will you, corporal? To tell the truth, I was just a little bit—"

He finished the sentence by shrugging his shoulders, and Bob, who knew what he meant by that, was about to assure him that he would say nothing in the hearing of the "boys" that would enable them to "get the laugh" on him, when George Ackerman broke in with—

"You had good reason to be alarmed, and this is not a matter to be dropped with an 'ah!' and an 'oh!' and a 'humph!' You are in great danger, if you only knew it. Those buffaloes are stampeded, and will not stop until they are all out of breath."

"Well, if they don't want to stop, let them run," said Bob. "Who cares? They don't owe us anything. They will of course turn aside when they see us."

"But they will not see you unless you do something to attract their attention," exclaimed George impatiently. "They will be in among us in five minutes more, and men and horses will be trampled into the ground like blades of grass. Wake up and do something, can't you? The safety of the camp depends upon you, and if you don't move, I will."

"Great Moses!" ejaculated Bob. He was thoroughly aroused by the earnest words of his companion, but having never been placed in a situation like this before, he did not know how to act. "You don't mean that—I never heard of—"

"Yes, I do mean that they will trample the whole camp to death unless you prevent it; and I don't care whether you ever heard of such a thing being done or not," cried George, seizing the corporal by the arm and shaking him as if he wanted to put a little energy into him.

"But what shall I do? Shall I order up the reserve and get the horses out of the way?"

"You haven't got time to get them out of the way. The buffaloes will be upon us before you could take half a dozen of them to a place of safety. Arouse the camp the first thing, and then call up a few good men to go out and split the herd the moment it comes in sight."

Bob, who was still in the dark, was about to ask how he should go to work to "split" the herd after he had selected the men, but George did not give him the opportunity. The rumbling of the approaching hoofs grew louder and louder, and every moment was precious. It sounded before them and to the right and left of them, indicating that the herd was an immense one, and that it was advancing with a front broad enough to overwhelm the entire camp. Knowing that no more time could be wasted in debating the matter, George unslung his Winchester and fired two shots into the air. The effect was almost magical. The camp, which had been so quiet a second before, was aroused into instant life and activity. Loud cries of "Indians!" and "Fall in!" arose on the still air, followed by blasts from the bugle and stern notes of command. The officer of the guard was promptly on the ground, and to him Bob reported that a herd of stampeded buffaloes was bearing down upon them. The announcement startled the lieutenant, but he acted with the greatest coolness. As fast as the men came up he ordered them back to take care of the horses—all except a dozen or so of the best soldiers known to him, whom he ordered to follow him. By the time he had taken up his position, which was on a little rise of ground about fifty yards from post No. 7, Captain Clinton came up. Taking in at a glance the arrangements which his subordinate had made to avert the terrible danger that threatened the camp, he left him and his picked men to carry out those arrangements or perish in the attempt, while he hastened back to see that the horses were well secured.

"Steady!" commanded Lieutenant Earle, speaking in his loudest tones, in order to make his voice heard above the roar of the threatening hoofs, which sounded like the noise made by an approaching hurricane. "We are here to conquer or die. If we don't split that herd they will trample us out of sight in the ground. We can do it if we are only cool enough to hold our position. Don't fire until I give the word, and then put in the shots as rapidly as you know how."

Bob's hair fairly stood on end, and not even the calm bearing of George Ackerman, who was constantly by his side and who knew their danger better than he did, or the lieutenant's assurance that the herd could be split if they did their full duty, could relieve Bob's mind of the positive conviction that he and his comrades were doomed to certain and speedy death. But his courage never faltered, and to show that he did not intend to allow himself to be outdone in steadiness even by a shoulder-strap, he walked up and kneeling beside his officer (the men in the front rank were all kneeling, so that those in the rear rank could shoot over their heads) waited for the order to fire.

Nearer came the terror-stricken buffaloes, louder grew the thunder of their hoofs, and, as if to add to the horror of the situation and to test the courage of the lieutenant and his devoted little band to the very utmost, the horses behind them began to grow unmanageable from fright and to struggle desperately to escape from their fastenings.

At length, after a few moments of dreadful suspense, the

time for action arrived. A rapidly-moving mass, which was plainly visible, owing to the fact that it was blacker than the darkness of the night, burst into view and bore down upon the camp and its little band of defenders. So loud was the noise made by their hoofs at this moment that the troopers did not hear the order to fire, which the lieutenant shouted out with all the power of his lungs; but they saw the flash of his revolver, and lost no time in opening a hot fire upon that portion of the herd which was directly in front of them. To Bob it seemed that the rapid discharges of their breech-loaders had no effect whatever. The black mass before him was as black and as dense, apparently, as it was when he first saw it, but, strange to say, instead of plunging upon him and his companions and trampling them out of all semblance to humanity, it seemed to remain stationary, although the deafening roar of those countless hoofs told him that the frantic herd had not in the least slackened its pace. In fact, his eyes and ears seemed to have suddenly become at "outs," for they did not endorse each other as they usually did. His eyes told him that his carbine was fired rapidly, for they showed him the flashes that followed the pulling of the trigger; but his ears took no note of the fact, for he could not hear the faintest report. The reason for this was, that the herd, having been split in two by the first volley, was moving by on each side of them with a roar and a rush that would have drowned the discharge of a section of artillery.

How long the buffaloes were in passing Bob never knew, for he took no note of time. It was probably not more than two or three minutes, but during that brief period he passed through an ordeal that he never could think of afterward without feeling the cold chills creep all over him. But he did not flinch, and neither did his companions. When the last of the buffaloes passed to the right and left of them, and the lieutenant jumped up and stretched his arms and legs as if to assure himself that he had not been stepped on anywhere, he found that not one of his men had moved from his place. The front rank was still kneeling, the rear rank was standing, and they were both as well aligned as they were before the firing commenced.

After ordering the front rank to rise, and bestowing upon them all a few hearty words of commendation, the lieutenant marched his men back to the camp, where they found some of their companions under arms, and the rest engaged in bringing in the horses and making them fast to the stable-lines. The animals were in such a state of alarm, and showed so strong a desire to run off with the retreating buffaloes, that Captain Clinton thought it advisable to put a strong guard over them for the rest of the night, with instructions to examine their fastenings every few minutes. When this guard had been detailed and the sentries had been changed, the rest of the troopers went back to their blankets.

Bob and George were proud of the part they had acted in saving the camp from destruction, and consequently when they spread their blankets beside one of the fires they were somewhat provoked to hear the man who was piling fresh fuel upon it attribute their narrow escape to "luck." But still there was nothing very surprising in this, for it not infrequently happens that a soldier stationed in one end of a camp does not know what is going on in the other end of it, especially in times of excitement. The same thing happens in a fight. A soldier may be able to give a clear statement of the part his company took in it, but he knows nothing of the general plan of the battle or of the number of the killed, wounded, captured or missing, until he has had time to talk the matter over with his comrades or to read a published account of it. During the war it was a common saying among the soldiers in the field that they never knew anything about the fights they had been in until they saw the papers.

"I have been on the Plains nearly three years," said the trooper who was punching up the fire, "and that was the first time I ever saw a herd of stampeded buffaloes."

"I never saw one," said another trooper. "I heard this one, but my horse kept me so busy that I couldn't take time to look at it."

"I had a fair view of it," said the one who had first spoken. "My horse was quiet enough after I got the bit between his teeth, so that I could manage him, and I stood up there by that farther fire and took it all in. I tell you, it was a sight!—a regular cataract of buffaloes a hundred feet wide, tumbling over a bank twenty feet high. I have always heard that when buffaloes become frightened and get to running they turn aside for nothing; but this night's experience gives the lie to all such stories, don't it? When they saw our camp they turned to the right and left, and crossed the stream above and below us, and never did us the least damage. Luck was on our side, wasn't it?"

"'Luck'!" repeated Bob in a tone of disgust; "I guess not. There were about a dozen men, of whom George Ackerman and I made two, who stood between you fellows and certain death. If we hadn't held our ground as if we had grown there, there wouldn't have been one of you left to tell the story of this night's work."

The troopers lying about the fire were greatly astonished at these words, and called for an immediate explanation. Bob told the story in a few words, adding, as he directed the attention of his auditors to George Ackerman, who was lying at his ease on his blanket,

"There's the fellow you have to thank for your 'luck.' Sprague heard them coming, and so did I after he called me out to his post, but we didn't know what it was until Ackerman told us.

Harry Castlemon

He was the one who alarmed the camp. I know I did something toward splitting that herd, for I could see the fire come out of my carbine and my cartridge-box is empty, but I never heard a report. I didn't hear anything but the thunder of those hoofs, and I shall hear it to my dying day."

"I wonder what started them?" said one of the troopers, after he and his companions had asked a few questions concerning the behavior of the various members of the squad. "Indians?"

"Probably they did," answered a sergeant, who just then came up to the fire to light his pipe, being unable to go to sleep until he had taken a smoke to quiet his nerves.

"Probably the Indians had nothing to do with it," said George. "Don't you know that a herd of buffaloes will feed within a mile or two of an Indian camp for days at a time, while half a dozen white men would scare them out of the country in less than an hour? Well, it's a fact."

"What is the reason for it?" asked Bob.

"The reason is to be found in the different modes of hunting them. The Indian, who depends largely upon them for food and clothing, kills no more of them during a run than the squaws can take care of. He hunts them almost altogether with the bow and arrow, which are not only very effective weapons at short range, but they make no noise to scare away the game. He hunts according to long-established rules, none but the best men in the tribe being permitted to take part in a run, and in this way the game is secured before the buffaloes get frightened enough to break into a stampede. The white man, who hunts principally for profit, keeps up the killing as long as he can hold the herd within range of his gun. He follows them persistently during the daytime, and at night lies in wait to shoot them as they come to the streams to quench their thirst. A buffalo is a very stupid animal, but, after all, it doesn't take him long to get some things through his head."

"Fresh, purty *fresh*!" murmured a voice.

George looked over his shoulders and saw the scout lying close by on his blanket. He had come up to the fire and arranged his bed without attracting the attention of any one.

"Do you think there is nobody in this party who knows anything except yourself?" demanded George.

"Well, no; judgin' by the way you sling your chin, you know it all," replied the scout.

"What do you suppose first put this herd in motion?" asked one of the troopers, who had not yet gained all the information he wanted.

"That's a question that nobody can answer unless he was on the ground and saw them start," answered George.—"You'll not dispute that, will you, Mose?—Our Texas cattle will often get stampeded by the sight of a little cloud of dust that is suddenly raised by the wind; or some night a careless herdsman may step between them and the fire and throw his shadow upon them; or some of the young and foolish members of a drove will fall to skylarking, and that will frighten the others, and the first thing you know they are all off like the wind. Buffaloes have just as little sense. My herdsman has told me that he has seen hundreds of them, when they were suffering for water, walk into a stream that was literally choked with the bodies of their companions who had been caught in the quicksand."

"Say," growled a drowsy trooper from his blanket, "suppose

you boys go somewhere and hire a hall?"

George laughed, and, taking the hint thus delicately thrown out, brought his lecture on buffaloes to a close. The remembrance of the thrilling scene through which he had just passed did not keep him awake. On the contrary, sleep came to his eyes almost immediately, and the last sound he heard as he was about to pass into the land of dreams was the subdued voice of the scout murmuring, "Fresh, very fresh!"

CHAPTER XI

TELEGRAPHING BY SMOKES

The camp was aroused at an early hour the next morning, and by the time it was fairly daylight breakfast had been disposed of and the column was again in motion. The firing-squad had brought down a goodly number of buffaloes in their efforts to split the herd—enough to furnish the whole camp with a hearty meal and to enable each trooper to carry two days' cooked rations in his haversack. During the first few miles of their march there was no trail for them to follow, all traces of the thieving Kiowas having been obliterated by the hoofs of the stampeded buffaloes; but this did not interfere with the movements of the scout, who, from the start, led the way at a rapid pace. He knew the general direction in which the trail led, and that was enough for him.

"Where do you think we shall pick it up again?" asked Captain Clinton of George, who rode by his side.

"Do you see that butte?" asked George in reply, directing the officer's attention to a single high peak in the distance, which marked the south-eastern boundary of the dreaded Staked Plains. "We shall not see another drop of water until we reach that mountain, and we shall find some traces of the Indians there, if we do not find them before."

"Purty fresh!" exclaimed the scout, who had overheard every word of this conversation.

"Well, if you know better, why don't you say so?" demanded George. "Every prediction I have made so far has turned out to be correct. Now, see how far I miss it when I tell you that the Indians camped beside that butte last night."

"Then we are gaining on them?" said the captain.

"We are," was the boy's confident reply. "And for the reason that we have followed a direct course and ridden rapidly, while the Indians took a roundabout way and moved slowly, being hampered by their stolen cattle."

George's calculations proved to be correct. About three o'clock in the afternoon they again took up the trail, and followed it at a gallop. They reached the peak just before dark, and found abundant evidence that the Indians had recently camped there. The troopers halted here too to get a little rest and a wink of sleep, but at nine o'clock they were once more on the move. The next halt was made about two in the morning, and at daylight they were again in their saddles and riding ahead as rapidly as ever. The trail led them along the borders of the Staked Plains, giving some of the troopers, who had never before scouted so far in this direction, their first view of that desolate region. A gloomy-looking place it was. As far as their eyes could reach they could see nothing but sandhills, with stunted weeds and clumps of grass which seemed to be struggling hard to maintain a foothold in the arid soil.

They had marched perhaps ten miles from their last camp when George Ackerman, who was riding by Captain Clinton's side, discovered something. He looked at it for a moment, and then called the officer's attention to it.

"They have begun their tricks at last," said he. "Do you see that dark streak out there in the grass? That's a new trail. There! Mose has discovered it, and is going out to see what it looks like."

Bringing the column to a halt, the captain, accompanied by George and some of the officers, rode forward to the place where the scout, who had got down from his horse, stood bending over the trail. After he had taken plenty of time in which to make his investigations, he straightened up to announce the result.

"Four of them varmints has gone this way, cap," said he. "They've left a plain trail, on purpose to coax you to foller 'em."

"They shall be gratified," answered the captain promptly. "As my party is larger than theirs, I can stand more divisions than they can. I would as soon whip them in detail as to whip them in a lump.—Earle, take a dozen men from your troop and follow it up."

"Very good, sir," replied the lieutenant.

"Have you brought your signal-code with you? All right! If you discover anything startling, send a courier to me with the fullest details. I will follow along after the main body. Be cautious, but at the same time keep moving, for we ought to be within striking distance of those rascals in a few hours more."

The lieutenant saluted and rode back to the column, drawing his sword as he went. Dropping the weapon behind the third column of fours, he gave the order. "The first three fours, right by twos—march! Column left—march!"

This brought the selected twelve alongside the new trail, which they at once began to follow up at a gallop, waving their caps to their comrades as they rode away. By selecting his men in this way the lieutenant did not happen to take Bob Owens, who rode farther back in the column. The young soldier, who was not in the habit of being slighted when there was anything of this kind going on, was both surprised and provoked at his officer; but he afterward thanked him for choosing his men as he did, and congratulated himself on having been left behind. Mr. Wentworth gazed longingly after the lieutenant, and sometimes seemed on the point of riding in pursuit of him; but he finally made up his mind to stay with the main column.

The troopers presently resumed the march, keeping up the same rapid pace as before, and in a few minutes lost sight of Lieutenant Earle and his party, who disappeared among the sandhills. The latter must have ridden very swiftly, for shortly after noon they were a long distance from the main body, their position being pointed out by a slender column of white smoke that suddenly arose in the air.

"That's them varmints, cap," said the scout, whose eye was quick to detect the signal. "They're talkin' to each other."

"I know there is somebody where that smoke comes from, but I am not sure that they are hostiles," replied Captain Clinton. "On the contrary, I am of the opinion that the men who built that fire want to talk to *me*. At any rate, I shall soon know."

As the captain said this he pulled his watch from his pocket with one hand, and with the other produced a note-book, which he held ready for reference. The column was not halted, but the eye of every man in it was fastened upon the distant smoke. When it had ascended to such a height that its top seemed lost in the clouds, it was suddenly cut loose from the ground by some mysterious agency, and floated off into space. A few seconds passed, and then two balloon-shaped clouds arose in quick succession from the same spot, and George took note of the fact that when the last one arose the captain looked at his watch. Another short interval elapsed, and then two more clouds arose, and finally two more; whereupon the captain gave his knee a ringing slap and consulted his note-book.

"I knew I couldn't be mistaken," said he. "That's from Earle, and he is about to communicate with me by courier.—Push ahead now, scout, for he is on a hot trail. Hallo! have you found another?" he added as the scout, instead of obeying the order to "push ahead," suddenly drew up his horse and threw himself from his saddle. "How many have gone off this time?"

"The same number," answered the scout, "an' they were goin' somewhar too, for their ponies were movin' at full jump when they turned off here. They're up to some trick or another, but I can't tell yet what it is."

"Then we must find out, for it is our business to look into these little things. I should like to know where this trail leads to, and I want—Let me see."

The captain turned about and ran his eye over the column, which came to a halt as soon as the commanding officer was seen to stop his horse. He seemed to be in a quandary, out of which he was helped almost immediately by the sight of a soldierly figure upon which his gaze rested for a moment.

"He's the man I want," said the captain aloud.—"Ackerman, will you tell Lieutenant Smith, who is now in command of Earle's troop, that I want to see Corporal Owens?"

"Certainly, sir. May I go with him?" replied George, who knew in a moment that there was something in the wind.

The captain nodded assent, and George galloped back to the column. When he returned Bob Owens rode at his side. The captain was writing—copying something upon a piece of paper from his note-book—but he stopped long enough to return Bob's salute, although he did not say anything to him. Seeing that the officer's horse was growing restive at the delay, and that by his constant pawing and tossing of his head he disturbed his rider, who did his writing while seated in the saddle, Bob dismounted and took the animal by the bridle, and the troopers who remained in column seized the opportunity to fill and light their pipes.

"There!" said the captain at length.—"Step up here, corporal, and I will explain this to you.—Ackerman, tell Lieutenant Smith to pick out twelve good men to follow this new trail."

By the time the lieutenant had received and obeyed this order, Captain Clinton, who was a fast talker, had told the corporal just what he wanted him to do, and explained to him the contents of the paper he had copied from his note-book; and Bob, who was quick to comprehend, had caught and weighed all his words as fast as they were uttered. He then put himself at the head of his men and led them away, George Ackerman riding by his side.

"Now we are off for another lark," exclaimed Carey as soon as he and his companions had left the column out of hearing. By some chance, he and Loring and Phillips had been selected to accompany Bob on every one of his expeditions, and as they had never failed to accomplish the object for which they were sent out, they began to think that there was nothing too hard for them to undertake.

"But this may not be so much of a 'lark' as you think," said Bob; and Carey afterward recalled the words when he found himself debarred from accompanying other scouting-parties on account of a painful wound in his sword-arm. "We are not out after deserters now, but Indians."

"What are you going to do with them if you find them?" asked Loring.

"I shall make things as lively for them as I can," replied Bob. "But I don't think I shall come up with them; and the captain doesn't expect me to. He is going to follow every trail and force the Indians to go back to their agency, whether they want to go or not; that is, unless we can overhaul them before they get there."

"I *know* we are not out on a 'lark,'" said George Ackerman. "What would you say if we had to go into camp to-night without water?"

"Gracious!" exclaimed Phillips, looking around at the sandhills, which now shut them in on all sides. "The prospect of finding a stream or a spring is not very flattering, is it? I wish we could find one now, for the water in my canteen is just ready to boil."

"You had better be careful of it," said George, "for it is much better than none at all."

"Is there any water to be found in this country?"

"Oh yes; and this trail will take us to it by the shortest route. An Indian can't live without water any more than we can, and he knows just where to find it."

"Say, George," exclaimed Bob suddenly, "didn't I hear Mose

say that when the four horses that made this trail turned off the *big* trail, they were going at full speed?"

George replied that he did say so.

"How did he know it?" continued Bob.

"By the looks of the tracks and the distance between them. When a horse is walking his hind foot covers about half the print made by his fore foot, and the tracks are from two and a half to three feet apart. When the horse is trotting the tracks are not so distinct, the one made by the fore foot being nearly covered up, and they are from seven to eight feet apart. When he is running the print of only one foot can be seen, as a general thing the ground about the tracks is considerably disturbed, and they are from seven to twelve feet apart."

If Carey and the rest of the squad did not learn to their entire satisfaction that they were not out on a picnic this time, the horses on which they were mounted certainly did, for before an hour had passed they were very much in need of water—so much so that Bob brought them down to a trot, and at last to a walk. At the end of another hour their riders began to suffer in the same way, and it was not long before every drop in their canteens, warm as it was, had disappeared. Whether it was the parched appearance of things around them; or the effects of the wind, which came into their faces as hot as a blast from a furnace; or the reflection of the sun's rays from the sandhills around them; or the sand itself, which arose in the air when disturbed by their horses' hoofs, and settled in their mouths and nostrils,—whether it was one or all of these causes combined that made them so very thirsty they did not think to inquire, but certain it was that they would have welcomed the discovery of a water-course more heartily now than at any other time during their march. Just how long this state of affairs was to continue they did not know, for there was not one among them who could tell whether water was five or twenty miles off. The only thing they could do was to follow the trail and await the issue of events with all the patience they could command.

After they had been separated from the main column for about three hours, two incidents happened which served to relieve the monotony of the march, and caused them, for the time being, to forget how uncomfortably hot and dusty and thirsty they were. As they were riding silently along behind George Ackerman, whose fast-walking nag had carried him some distance in advance of the squad, they saw him draw rein all of a sudden and raise his hand with a warning gesture. Then he backed his horse under cover of a convenient sandhill, and pulling his field-glass from the case he carried slung over his shoulder, he levelled it at some object that had attracted his attention, but which could not be seen by the troopers.

Bob at once ordered a halt, and rode forward to inquire into the matter. When he reached George's side he found himself on the outskirts of a sort of basin in the plain, which looked as though it might have been scooped out by the wind. It was covered with sand, and dotted here and there with little bunches of yellow grass and weeds. On the opposite side of this basin, which was perhaps a mile and a half wide, was a single horseman, who was riding toward them at a rapid pace.

"I couldn't make out, at that distance, whether he was a friend or foe, so I thought it best to warn you," said George.

"That was all right, of course. Can you make him out with your glass?"

"Very plainly. He's a soldier—one of Lieutenant Earle's men, probably."

Harry Castlemon

"That's just who he is," exclaimed Bob after he had taken a look at the horseman through the field-glass. "I know him. That signal-smoke we saw just before we left the column was sent up to inform the captain that Earle had despatched a courier to him with some important news, and now we will find out what it is.—Come on, fellows," he added, waving his hand to the squad; "it is one of our own company, boys."

Bob and his companion rode out in plain view, and a few seconds later the troopers joined them. Their sudden appearance must have astonished the approaching courier, and perhaps alarmed him too, for he pulled up his horse with a jerk, and, shading his eyes with his hand, gazed at them long and earnestly. They waved their caps to reassure him, and in a few minutes he came up. The first words he uttered showed that he had already had quite enough of scouting in the Staked Plains.

"Did anybody ever see so dreary a hole as this?" said he as he lifted his cap and drew his handkerchief across his forehead—"nothing but sandhills as far as you can see, and one looks so much like another that a fellow don't know how to shape a course. It must be just fearful in here when the wind blows.—I say, corporal, where am I? and what are you doing out here?"

"I can't answer your first question, for I don't know myself," answered Bob. "I was sent out to follow a new trail we found just after you sent up that smoke. What was the meaning of it?—Carey, climb up to the top of that sandhill and tell us if you can see anything."

"Lieutenant Earle sent up that smoke to let the captain know that he was about to send him some news," replied the horseman; "and I don't see why the captain didn't send up a reply, for I don't know where to find him."

"I will point out his position as near as I can before you leave us," said Bob. "Is that news of any importance?"

"I should say it was," exclaimed the courier. "We've struck it hot, I tell you. On the banks of a little stream we found somewhere off in that direction—"

"Look here, Aleck!" exclaimed Loring; "I thought that canteen of yours looked as though it had been dipped in water not so *very* long ago. Why don't you pass it around? We haven't got a drop left."

"Is that so?" said the courier, who promptly unslung his canteen. "You are welcome to it, but touch it easy, so that everybody can have a taste, and don't forget to save some for Carey.—As I was saying, on the banks of that stream the scout discovered the tracks of little boots."

The troopers all uttered exclamations when they heard this, and Loring was so anxious to hear more that he forgot he was thirsty, and after holding the canteen in his hand for a moment passed it to a comrade without tasting of its contents.

"Mr. Wentworth acted as though he thought he ought to go with Lieutenant Earle's squad, and when he hears that he will be sorry that he stayed behind," observed Bob.

"Won't he, though!" said the courier.

"I suppose there is no doubt that the tracks were made by his boys?" said George.

"None whatever. How could there be? The Indians have no other prisoners with them."

"They have none that we know of," said George. "But as they visited other ranches, they may have taken other boys captive."

"How do you know that they did visit other ranches?" demanded the courier. "Mr. Wentworth didn't say anything about it in my hearing."

"Nor in mine, either," replied George. "But he did say in my hearing that he had lost not more than half a dozen horses, and the trail shows that they have more than fifty with them."

"Well," said the courier, looking down at the horn of his saddle in a brown study, "if that's the case, the Indians may have—No, they didn't, either," he added, brightening. "Mr. Wentworth told the colonel, in Lieutenant Earle's hearing, that the Indians jumped down on his ranche just after he had finished mending his oldest boy's boots. He put a patch on each one of them just under the ball of the foot, and those patches showed in the tracks."

"Ah!" exclaimed George, "that will pass for evidence."

"At any rate," continued the courier, "I was ordered to tell the captain that we were on the trail of the party who had the children. That's all the news I have, I believe.—What shall I tell the captain for you, corporal?"

"Say to him that you found me following up my trail as fast as the condition of my horses would permit," answered Bob. "It is as plain as daylight, and if I could only get some water now and then, I could follow it at a gallop.—What is it, Carey?"

"A smoke away off to the south-east," replied the soldier, who was lying flat on the top of the nearest sandhill.

Bob at once dismounted and made his way up the hill, followed by George and the courier. They did not expose their full height to view, but crept up on their hands and knees, and when they reached the top pulled off their caps before they looked over it. They knew that Indians, when they are retreating, always leave some of their number to watch the trail, and they adopted these precautions in order to avoid discovery by these rear-guards should there chance to be any in the neighborhood. The reflection of the sun's rays from the brass ornaments on their caps would have been seen by a watchful Indian at an almost incredible distance.

"I see the smoke," said Bob, pulling from his pocket the paper which Captain Clinton had given him—"Where is your watch, George? Now look for the signal."

The smoke, like the one Lieutenant Earle had sent up a few hours before, ascended in a straight, slender column for a few seconds, and then floated away out of sight. A few seconds later three little columns, shaped like the clouds which are thrown out by the discharge of a cannon, arose in the air in quick succession, followed after a little delay by three others. Bob waited and watched, but as no more clouds appeared, he knew that the signal had been made. The next thing was to find out what it meant.

"George," said he, "after those first three smokes appeared how long was it before the others were seen?"

"Just thirty seconds," replied the time-keeper.

Bob ran his eye over the paper he held in his hand, and presently found the following, which he read aloud: "Three smokes, followed at the interval of half a minute by three others, are intended to point out the position of the signalling-party."—"There you are!" said he, turning to the courier. "Fix in your mind the place from which that smoke arose, and then travel a little to the north of it, so as to allow for the captain's progress, and you will find him."

"How far away was that smoke?" asked the courier as he and his companions crept back down the hill.

"Fifteen miles," replied George.

"Whew! Well, I'll get there if I can. Who's got my canteen? Why, you have left some in it!" he added as one of the squad handed him the article in question. "Don't any of you want another taste?"

Yes, there were plenty there who could have drained the canteen to the last drop and then called for more, but knowing that the courier would have need of it before he had galloped fifteen miles under that broiling sun with the hot wind blowing upon him, they all declared that they had had enough.

After Carey and Loring had moistened their parched lips the courier sprang upon his horse and waved his farewell, while Bob and his men, feeling somewhat refreshed, took up the trail again and followed it at a trot.

CHAPTER XII

ANOTHER FEATHER FOR BOB'S CAP

The second diversion of which we have spoken occurred about an hour after Lieutenant Earle's courier left them. It was nothing more nor less than the discovery of the fact that the party of whom they were in pursuit had been joined by another warrior, whose pony's tracks came from the direction in which the lieutenant was supposed to be scouting. Bob and his men did not seem to attach much importance to this, but George did. He looked the ground over very carefully, and reached conclusions that astonished himself.

"Bob Owens," said he in a low tone as they resumed the march, "you've got another chance to put a feather in your hat—a big one, too. Lieutenant Earle will never rescue Mr. Wentworth's boys, but you can if you're smart."

Bob, who always listened in the greatest amazement (and with some incredulity, too, it must be confessed) to his friend's predictions, could only look the surprise he felt. How any one, by simply looking at a pony's track, could tell what a party of men whom he had never seen were going to do, he could not understand.

"To begin with," continued George, "our Indians expected to

have an addition made to their party, and they expected also that it would be made just where it *was* made. How do I know that? By the looks of things. The ponies were all huddled together in one place, and they must have stood there a good while, judging by the stamping they did. Their riders must have dismounted there, for I saw the prints of their moccasins in the sand. I noticed also that the side of the nearest sandhill had been disturbed, and that told me that one of their number had climbed up there to watch for the expected warrior."

"Perhaps he was watching for us," suggested Bob.

"If he was, he wouldn't have watched for us with his feet, would he?" demanded George.

"'With his feet'?" echoed Bob.

"Yes. He would have been more likely to watch for us with his eyes."

"How do you know that he didn't?"

"Because he climbed up on our side of the hill, and that would have exposed his whole body to our view if we had been anywhere within sight of him. His eyes were turned the other way; that is, in Lieutenant Earle's direction. He wasn't afraid of being seen by us, but he took all due precautions to conceal himself from the gaze of any one who might happen to come that way from Lieutenant Earle's command; for near the place where the ponies were standing I saw the tufts of grass he had pulled up to tie around his head."

"Well, I am beat!" exclaimed Bob.

"What beats you?"

"You do: I didn't see any of those things."

"Probably you didn't, for the reason that you didn't look for them. You see, I have passed a good many years on the Plains, and I have learned that eternal vigilance is the price of a cowboy's life and liberty. When his scalp depends upon the correct reading of such signs as those which I have just described to you, he is not often caught napping. My long association with Zeke, whose eyes seemed to be everywhere, has got me into the habit of keeping my own eyes open. Probably there were other things there that would have been perfectly plain to Zeke or Mountain Mose which I didn't see.

"Now, of course I don't *know* that this new warrior brought Mr. Wentworth's children with him when he came over to join our Indians, but everything seems to point that way. One of the proofs—and the strongest, in my humble opinion—is found in the fact that the Indians allowed their captives to dismount on the banks of that stream the courier told us of. I am inclined to believe that they went farther than that, and compelled the boys to walk in the mud and leave their tracks there."

"I don't see why they did that," observed Bob. "I should think they would want to keep everybody from knowing where the boys were."

"So they would if they had intended to keep the boys with them, but they did not. This is their plan, as near as I can get at it; and in order to make my explanation clearer I will call the party of which Lieutenant Earle is in pursuit No. 1, that which we want to find No. 2, and that the captain is following up No. 3. The warriors in No. 1 are doubtless the best mounted of all the raiders. When they separated from the main body they left a broad trail, so that they could be easily followed, taking the children with them, and leaving now and then a sign of their presence, for no other purpose than to coax the captain to follow them with his whole force. As soon as they reached a piece of rocky ground, where a pony's feet would leave no track, one of their number picked up the boys and brought them over here, where party No. 2 was waiting for him. Those he left behind will show themselves to Lieutenant Earle occasionally, and perhaps open a little fight with him, just to induce him to continue the pursuit. Party No. 3 will drive the stock ahead as fast as possible, and get away with it if they can; but if they find that they are likely to be overtaken, they will drop the cattle and do everything they can to keep the captain on their trail, so as to give party No. 2 a chance to escape with the prisoners. Now, that's a long story, and no doubt it is a hard one to believe; but I don't think I am far from right when I tell you that it is quite in your power to carry off the honors of this expedition. Captain Clinton will have his hands full until he recovers that stock; so will Lieutenant Earle as long as he follows those will-o'-the-wisps in front of him; and to you will be left the duty, as well as the privilege, of looking out for the safety of Mr. Wentworth's little boys."

"Whew!" panted Bob, who was very much impressed, although not wholly convinced, by his companion's clear and forcible reasoning. "Then I am the chief man in this scout, am I? Suppose—I say, just *suppose*—I should be lucky enough to rescue those boys alive and unharmed, what would the fellows say? What would Mr. Wentworth say?"

"The boys would cheer you, and you would win Mr. Wentworth's everlasting gratitude," replied George. "But, Bob, the prisoners have not been rescued yet, and I warn you that unless you are as sly as a fox you will be the means of their death. If the Indians discover you, and find themselves unable to escape, their very first act will be to kill those boys."

"Good gracious!" exclaimed Bob, dropping his reins upon the horn of his saddle and pulling off his cap with one hand while he scratched his head vigorously with the other. "*Good gracious!* The captain never thought of that when he sent me off with this squad, did he? George, the responsibility is too heavy for me. I think I'll ask the captain where he is, and then go and report to him."

"That wouldn't be a very smart trick," protested George. "You would not only be taken to task for wasting valuable time, but the Indians, seeing a smoke that they couldn't understand arise on their trail, would take the alarm at once, and you would lose a fine chance of distinguishing yourself."

"Don't you suppose they saw the smoke that Lieutenant Earle sent up?"

"Of course they did—the captain's too. Those same smokes were a good thing for us, for I am of the opinion that they threw our party off their guard by leading them to believe they are not pursued. You mustn't send up a smoke along this trail if you want to catch those Indians. What are your orders, anyhow?"

"To follow the trail until I am recalled or until the Indians throw me off entirely," replied Bob.

"Then don't you see that you would be disobeying orders by marching your squad back to the column without a recall?" asked George. "You would surely get yourself into trouble by doing that, and besides, you would be hauled over the coals for not taking better care of your men and horses. They couldn't stand twenty miles more to-night without a rest, and how much of a rest could they get here in this oven, with no grass or water? Don't do it, Bob."

Harry Castlemon

"But the prisoners—just think of the prisoners!" exclaimed the perplexed corporal. "I don't want to feel that I am responsible for any harm that may befall them."

"I don't see how you are going to shirk it."

"Well, will you take command?"

"Certainly not," answered George quickly. "Don't confess your incapacity by surrendering your authority. Besides, a scout never commands—he only advises; and I will help you in that way all I can. Go on, and say that you will do your best."

"I will," said Bob, slamming his cap upon his head and seating himself firmly in his saddle. "If we can only place ourselves in a position to cover those boys, the Indians will not have a chance to touch them, I'll bet you. My men are all good marksmen."

"And I am a tolerable one myself," said George. "A single hair of those boys' heads is worth the lives of all the Indians that ever saw the Staked Plains, and if it becomes necessary to shoot in their defence, I am ready. There is a high sandhill, and if you will stop here for a few minutes I will go up and see if I can discover anything."

Bob raised his hand to halt the squad, and George swung himself out of his saddle. His first care was to lay aside his cap and rifle, and his next to pull up a quantity of grass and weeds to be used as a screen. With these in one hand and his field-glass in the other he crept slowly to the top of the sandhill, and, holding the screen a few inches above the ground, he pushed his field-glass under it and looked around.

"Aha!" was his mental exclamation, "I shall have good news to carry back to the boys. There's a deep gully about five miles off, and there must be a stream of water running through it, or else those willows would not be growing there. I wish we had got here an hour earlier, for then I should have had daylight to aid me in making my observations. The Indians probably halted in that gully a few hours ago, and the question to be decided now is—Hallo! If that isn't smoke rising among those trees, what is it? And didn't that little cluster of bushes over there on the top of that hill shift its position just now?"

George's heart beat wildly as he propounded these inquiries to himself. He took another long look, and then with a very slow and gradual motion he deposited his screen upon the sand and backed down to the plain. His stealthy movements told the troopers that he had seen something.

"Corporal," said he as they rode up to him, "before you ask any questions let me suggest that you order your men to remove their sabres as quietly as possibly."

Bob quickly unhooked his own sabre from his belt, and looked at his men, who made all haste to follow his example. They knew that there could be but one reason for this order. A steel scabbard hanging by the side of a careless rider will strike against his spurs with every step his horse takes, or rattle against his leg as the trooper walks about, giving out a clear ringing sound that will betray his presence to foes far less watchful and sharp-eared than Indians.

"So we have run them into their holes, have we?" said Bob when he had acted upon George's suggestion.

"That remains to be seen. They are camped about five miles from here, and one of their lookouts is watching the trail."

The troopers looked at Bob as if to ask what he was going to do about it, and Bob, who had as little idea of the orders he ought to give under the circumstances as he had of the Greek language, looked at George. The latter did not say anything, for he wanted the troopers to hold fast to their belief that the corporal was able to act for himself in any and every emergency; but he gave his friend a look that was plainly understood.

"Dismount," commanded Bob; "we'll rest here until we can determine upon something. Let every man keep fast hold of his horse, for a neigh from one of them would make dough of our cake in a little less than no time. Eat and whisper as much as you please, but—"

"Don't smoke," put in George.

"Oh, Moses!" ejaculated the troopers in subdued tones.

"An Indian will smell smoke from a pipe or a camp-fire a long distance," added George.

"Then keep your pipes in your pockets, where they can't do any mischief," said Bob.—"George, I'd like to take a look at that camp."

George at once led the way up the hill, but when he neared the top he said in a whisper,

"Perhaps you had better trust to my eyes instead of your own; not but that you can see as far as I can, but you might be a little careless in handling that screen, and the least false motion on your part would be seen by that lookout, whose eyes are as good as a telescope."

"All right!" replied Bob, who wondered what he should have done if George had not been there to advise him. "What shall we do?"

"Let me take another look, and then I will talk to you."

So saying, George crept back to the top of the hill and looked under his screen as before. It was rapidly growing dark, but he could see that the sentry still kept his position, and that the camp-fire was burning brightly.

"They do not stand in the least fear of pursuit," said he as he backed down to Bob's side, "but they have taken measures to prevent surprise, as they always do when they are on the war-path."

"How long do you suppose that sentry will stay there?"

"Just as long as his friends stay in the gully. I do not mean by that that this particular Indian will act as lookout all the time, but that some member of the party will be constantly on the watch."

The first thing to be done was to decide upon a plan of operations, and this took a good deal of hard thinking, for there was a good deal depending upon it. George made the most of the suggestions, and Bob accepted every one of them without argument. The camp was to be attacked as soon as they could get within reach of it: both were agreed upon that. Bob advised a surround, in order to prevent the escape of any of the Indians; but George objected, urging as a reason for his objections that no one but an Indian could work his way through those thick bushes and trees without making a good deal of noise, and that would knock the whole thing in the head.

"Don't be too ambitious," said he. "Don't try to grab too big a handful, and so run the risk of losing everything. Keep your men near you, so that you can have an eye on every one of them. Look out for the boys; and if by so doing you give the Indians a chance to escape, as you will most likely, let them go and welcome."

An immediate advance having been resolved upon, and the part that each man was to play in the coming fight (provided the Indians decided to make a fight of it) having been thoroughly discussed, Bob and his companion returned to the place where they had left the troopers. The former issued his orders in a few brief words, and in a very short space of time eight barefooted men, armed only with their carbines and revolvers, were drawn up in line ready to do his further bidding; while the four troopers who were to be left behind to hold the horses and to take care of the sabres, shoes and stockings which their lucky comrades had thrown upon the ground, listened with as good grace as they could to a few parting words from their corporal.

"Now, boys," said the latter, "keep quiet and don't smoke. We have been following the trail of only five Indians, but we don't know how many may have joined them since they went into camp; so you must hold yourselves in readiness for any emergency. Keep a good lookout for the signal, and if you don't see it by the time the moon rises, which will be about midnight, take care of yourselves. Draw as straight a course for the column as you can, and tell the boys, when you find them, that the reds got the best of us while we were trying to do our duty. Good-bye.—Lead on, George."

Although our hero had passed his life amid scenes of danger, and more than once listened to the sound of hostile bullets (that was during the "neighborhood row" of which we have spoken in the first volume of this series), he had never before taken part in a scout after Indians, and it may be readily imagined that Bob's parting words did not serve to encourage him in any great degree. Bob seemed to think that there was a possibility that their attempted surprise might end in utter defeat. The bare thought was enough to make George's hair stand on end, but it did not make him lose any of the sympathy he felt for the boy-captives or falter in his resolve to do all he could toward effecting their release. In obedience to Bob's order to "lead on" he raised his rifle to his shoulder and glided off into the darkness, the troopers following in single file. Before he had marched half a mile Bob hurried up and placed himself by his side.

"Say, George," he whispered, "you are not going toward the camp. If you follow this course, you will miss it by half a mile or more."

"I don't want to go toward the camp," was the reply. "We must circle around so as to come up in the rear of that sentry, who, as I told you, will stay on the top of that hill as long as his friends stay in the gully."

"Do you think we can capture him without alarming the others?"

"We are not going to try; at least, I sha'n't advise it. If we can save the boys, we ought to be satisfied. That sentry will dig out as soon as he scents danger, and all we can do is to let him go."

"How awful still it is, and how fearful dark!" continued Bob. "I hope you won't get confused and miss your way."

"There is no danger of that," replied George confidently. "I can see the stars, and they are as good as a compass to me. I have often travelled by them, and they have never fooled me yet."

"Where are the wolves, I wonder?" said Bob, who was so

impatient and so highly excited that he could not long hold his peace. "They keep up their unearthly howls every night when we wish them a thousand miles away, but now, when a yelp from one of them would be a relief, they don't put in an appearance."

"And I am glad of it," said George. "Don't you know that a pack of wolves are the best sentries a camping-party can have?"

Yes, Bob said he was aware of that fact.

"Well," continued George, "don't you see that the little breeze there is stirring is blowing from us toward the camp? If there were any wolves around, they would probably be on the other side of the gully, for it would be a waste of time for them to prowl around here among these sandhills, where they couldn't find even a rabbit to eat. The moment they caught our wind they would scamper off, and then 'Good-bye, prisoners.' I wish I knew where those Indians have staked out their ponies, for I stand more in fear of them than I do of that sentry. If we should get to windward of them, they would kick up a rumpus directly."

The longer Bob talked with George the more clearly the difficulties attending his undertaking seemed to stand but before him, and the greater grew his anxiety and impatience. If his attempt to surprise the Indian camp failed, there was no telling when Mr. Wentworth's boys would be heard of again. If it suited their captors to spare their lives, they would doubtless be sold to some band who lived at a great distance from the agency, and who would take the greatest pains to keep their existence a profound secret. If they were ever given up at all, it would only be after that particular band had been soundly thrashed for some outrage, and then they would be brought forward as an element in the "peace negotiations," their captors demanding a heavy ransom and taking great credit to themselves for surrendering them. But this might not happen for years, and during that time a great many things might happen to the boys. They might become so completely broken down by cruel treatment that their death would be a blessing, or else so thoroughly infatuated with the Indian mode of life that, if left to themselves, they would choose to go back to the wigwams of their savage masters rather than return to the home of their father.

"It's now or never," said Bob to himself after he had thought the matter over. "I don't wonder that Mr. Wentworth feels so spiteful, for if these Indians are not killed during this scout, they will never be punished for what they have done to him. The government is too tender-hearted to touch them, and if Mr. Wentworth takes the law into his own hands, he will be sure to suffer for it. They will go back to their agency to grow fat on government grub and be kept warm in winter by government blankets; and their agent, in order to prevent an investigation that might take a few dollars out of his pocket, will be ready to swear that they have never been off their reservation. I wonder how he would feel if he saw his own children carried into captivity?"

For two long hours the weary troopers continued the march, stopping for rest only when Bob and George climbed some sandhill to reconnoitre the ground before them. The deep silence that brooded over the Staked Plains was almost oppressive. The bare feet of the troopers gave out no sound as they sank into the yielding sand, and all that could be heard was their labored breathing as they walked behind their leader, trusting implicitly to his guidance. They never uttered a word, but Bob's impatience and nervousness would have kept his tongue in constant motion had it not been for George, who gave him an energetic prod in the ribs whenever he showed a disposition to become colloquial. He

Harry Castlemon

felt that he must do something pretty soon or sink under his burden of responsibility, which seemed to grow heavier the longer he walked; consequently, when George stopped all of a sudden and silently pointed his finger at a dense wall of trees that ran across their path, his delight knew no bounds. The ravine in which the Indians were encamped was close in front of them. The murmuring of the waterfall which came up from its wooded depths was a pleasant sound to his ears, but he and his troopers had much to do before they could quench their thirst at that rippling stream.

CHAPTER XIII

HE WINS IT FAIRLY

As it was not necessary to waste any precious time in giving verbal orders, a complete code of signals having been decided upon before they left their horses, George at once threw himself upon his hands and knees, and worked his way along the edge of the bluff until he reached a position directly above the camp, the location of which was pointed out by a little blaze, scarcely larger, apparently, than the flame of a candle. He looked in vain for the sentry, and would have given something handsome if there had been some one at hand to tell him just where he was.

"If he still holds his position on the top of that sandhill, we are all right," said George to himself, "but if he has taken the alarm, we are all wrong. In that case the Indians have done one of two things: they have either made ready to ambush us, or else they have fled, taking their prisoners with them. Well, we shall soon know, for here goes for the fight that none of us may ever come out of alive."

As these thoughts passed through George's mind he seized Bob's waist-belt and gave it two jerks, which meant "Follow me." Then he crept back along the line, and as he passed each trooper he took him by the arm and pulled him around, so that his head pointed toward the camp-fire. This meant a movement by the right flank. After this he and Bob placed themselves in the centre of the line, the men giving way right and left to make room for them, and at a given signal Bob stuck his elbow into the ribs of the trooper to the left of him, while George in a similar manner admonished the one on the right of himself; and the advance began, the guide being centre. We mean by this that the men on Bob's left kept themselves in their proper place in line by touching the shoulder of the man next on their right, while those on George's right hand kept within easy reach of the men next on their left, each member of the line moving no whit slower or faster than the guides in the centre, Bob and George. If *they* stopped and listened and tried to peer through the bushes in front of them to obtain a view of the camp, the whole line stopped and listened and peered. When the guides advanced the troopers did the same, their movements being conducted without a whisper, and with such extreme caution that scarcely a leaf was heard to rustle. It took them almost an hour to descend the bluff, which was probably not more than a hundred feet in height, but the sight that greeted them when the final halt was made more than repaid them for all their toil. They had crept up within less than a dozen yards of the fire, and the camp and all its inmates were in plain view of them.

Their first care was to find the boys, and the next to ascertain the number and position of their adversaries. The boys were there, lying side by side on a bed of leaves, with their arms thrown around each other, and wrapped in slumber as peaceful, apparently, as ever came to their eyes while they were safe under their father's roof. Every one of the troopers shut his lips tightly at the sight of them, and half a dozen cocked carbines were pointed over their unconscious heads, ready to send to kingdom-come the first thing in the shape of a Kiowa that dared approach them. They were not protected in any way from the night air save by the branches of the trees which waved gently above them, while every one of the four Indians who were lying around them was wrapped up head and ears in a quilt or blanket which he had stolen during the raid.

One sweeping glance was enough to enable Bob and George to take in all these little details, and it is scarcely necessary to say that they were highly elated over the promise of success which the situation seemed to hold out to them. Bob would have been a little better satisfied if he could have seen any way of taking the Indians alive, and so making a "finished job of it," as he afterward told his friend George; but, knowing that this was entirely beyond his power, he was about to give the signal to advance when a most unexpected interruption occurred. They heard the snapping of twigs behind them, accompanied by a slight rustling among the leaves, such as might be made by some heavy body working its way cautiously through the thick undergrowth. The astonished troopers hugged the ground closely, holding their breath in suspense; and in a second more, without a single footstep being audible, the bushes parted and the form of an Indian warrior could be dimly seen through the darkness.

"Beyond a doubt it is the sentry coming in to call his relief," thought Bob. "*Now*, how am I going to act? Shall I let him go into the camp, or not?"

Without pausing an instant, the Indian, all unconscious of danger, approached the line, and might have passed through it between Bob and Carey without discovering anything to excite his suspicions, had not the former, acting upon the impulse of the moment, made up his mind that he would not go back to his comrades without at least one prisoner to reward him for his long and tiresome scout. Throwing out his arm, he caught the warrior around the legs and lifting him

Harry Castlemon

from the ground threw him upon his back. He fell across Carey and Loring, both of whom turned like lightning and seized him, one trying to secure his arms, so that he could not draw a weapon, and the other taking him by the throat. Everything was done quickly, but not quickly enough to shut off the wild yell with which the captive Indian awoke the echoes of the gully. Seeing that all further attempts at concealment were useless, Bob and George jumped to their feet.

"Forward with a cheer!" yelled the former. "Cover the boys, everybody."

This last order was hardly necessary, for each individual member of the squad had secretly resolved to do that very thing, leaving his companions to act as they pleased.

The Indians were wide awake and moving before their unlucky comrade's yell had fairly left his lips. So quickly did they spring to their feet that the troopers might have thought, if they had been allowed time to think at all, that the savages had been merely keeping up an appearance of sleep, so as to be ready to jump from their blankets at the very first note of alarm. So well schooled were they, and so ready to act, and to act quickly and intelligently in any emergency, that they did not hesitate an instant. They did not even look to see from which way the danger that threatened them was coming, but made a simultaneous rush for their captives, intending, no doubt, to carry them away if they could, or to kill them if they found themselves surrounded so that they could not escape. But no Indian's hand touched those boys again that night. Three of them fell dead before they had fairly left their tracks, and the other, taking warning by their fate, dived into the bushes in much the same way that a boy takes a "header" from a log, and got safely off, in spite of the bullets which whistled about his ears and scattered the leaves all over him. The troopers knew that he had got off unhurt, because there was no blood on the trail which George took up the next morning and followed to the place where the Indians had left their horses—a little glade about a quarter of a mile from the camp in which grass was abundant and water easy of access.

George at once made his way to the side of the captives, who were sitting up on their bed of leaves, rubbing their eyes and looking about in a bewildered sort of way, and throwing his arm around them spoke soothing and encouraging words in their ears; while Bob, after ordering one of his men to mend the fire, seized a brand from it and ran back to see what had become of Carey and Loring. The fight was over, and Carey was growling lustily over a wound in his arm which the slippery savage had inflicted upon him, having managed in some mysterious way to gain momentary possession of his knife; but Loring was unharmed and the Indian was insensible. He had been knocked out of time by a vicious whack from the butt of a carbine held in the hands of the enraged Carey. The blow was not, however, as effective as the trooper intended it should be, for it had expended a good deal of its power upon the bushes which happened to be in the way, and instead of sending the Indian out of the world altogether, it had only stunned him. He was powerless now. His hands were securely confined by Loring's carbine-sling, and the latter, having passed the Indian's blanket under his arms and brought the ends together behind his back, was ready to drag his captive into camp.

"I am no slouch—there isn't a boy in the troop, young or old, who can take my measure on the ground—but if this fellow gave us a fair specimen of an Indian's way of rough-and-tumble fighting, I don't want to get hold of any more Indians.—He was a hard one, wasn't he?" said Loring, appealing to his wounded comrade, who grunted out an emphatic assent. "He didn't seem to be so very strong, but he was just a trifle quicker than chain-lightning, and as slippery and wiry as—as—Why, an eel isn't nowhere alongside of him."

"I wish I had whacked him over the head before he gave me this prod," said Carey, shaking his fist at the unconscious object of his wrath. "It's my sword-arm too, and I'll just bet that the doctor won't let me go on another scout for a month."

With Bob's aid the Indian was dragged into camp, and thrown down there as if he had been a sack of corn. The fire was burning brightly (an Indian builds a small fire and gets close to it, while a white man builds a big one and backs away from it), the bodies of the slain warriors had been dragged into the bushes out of sight, and their weapons, saddles and bridles, which the troopers intended to carry back to the fort with them as trophies of their prowess, had been collected and deposited in a safe place.

George had been devoting himself to the boys, who did not seem to be at all afraid, and were by no means so excited as he was. Their astonishing courage called forth the unbounded admiration of the troopers, and the pert answers they gave to the questions that were asked them made them smile.

"Say, Bob, if you want to see what Texas boys are made of, come here," said George. "The older one answers to the name of Sheldon, and the little fellow is Tommy. Sheldon says that if his brother had been a little older and stronger the Indians never would have taken them to their village, for they would have killed them and made their escape."

"Humph!" grunted Carey, whose wound seemed to put him

in very bad humor.

"What makes you say that?" demanded Bob, turning upon him somewhat sharply. "Don't you know that such things have been done before now?"

"By boys?" asked Carey.

"Yes, by boys," replied Bob.

"No, I don't know it," said the wounded trooper.

"It's a matter of history, any way," said George. "Two brothers, John and Henry Johnson, aged respectively thirteen and eleven years of age, were captured by two Delaware Indians on Short Creek, West Virginia, in October, 1788. That very night they killed their captors by shooting one and tomahawking the other."

"Did they get away?" asked Sheldon eagerly.

"Yes, sir, they got away. Now, I want to ask you a few questions—and, Bob, I want you to pay attention to his replies.—Where have you been to get so much mud on your boots?"

"Why, back there in the plains we came to a little bayou, and the banks of it was all muddy; and the Injins they pulled us off the ponies and made us walk into all that there mud, and then they laughed at us because we didn't like it," answered the boy; and his ludicrous display of rage over the indignity that had been put upon himself and his brother made the troopers smile again.

"Go on," said George. "What did you do next?"

"Well, they took us out of the mud after a while, the Injins did, and then one of 'em he took us on a pony and rode off by himself until he found this party; and we've been with them ever since."

"What did I tell you?" exclaimed George, hitting Bob a back-handed slap on the chest. "What do you think of my guessing now?"

"I think you are pretty good at it," answered Bob. "And seeing you *are*, I wish you would try your hand in a new line. Suppose you take a couple of men with you, and all our canteens and coffee-pots, and guess your way down the bluff to the stream, and bring us back a supply of water? We'll have a good fire going by the time you return, and then we'll boil a cup of coffee."

"I'll do it," said George readily.

"And while you are guessing, guess at the probable movements of that Indian who got away," continued Bob. "Will he be likely to trouble us to-night?"

"He will not," was the confident reply. "Our party is too large. He will make the best of his way home, you may depend upon it."

While George and the two troopers whom Bob detailed to accompany him were gone after the water, those who remained in camp were not idle. One bound up Carey's wounded arm, another brought in a bountiful supply of fire-wood, others stood guard, and one assisted the corporal in collecting a quantity of leaves and light branches, and went out with him to signal to the four men who had been left behind with the horses. They readily found the hill which had served as a lookout-station for the warrior who was now a captive in their hands; and they knew it when they found it, for there was the pile of bushes through which he had looked while watching the trail, and the print of his body in the sand. A fire was speedily lighted on the summit, and kept burning brightly to guide the absent troopers to the captured camp. That little beacon shining through the darkness must have been a welcome sight to their eyes, for it told of the complete success of their companions and of the rest and water that were to be found where they were.

When George returned to the camp after nearly half an hour's absence he found the fire blazing cheerily, and the two rescued boys, who seemed almost exhausted by their long journey, sleeping soundly beside it, covered by a quilt which some kind-hearted trooper had thrown over their shoulders. The troopers were laughing heartily but silently at Carey and Loring, who seemed to bear their merriment with very bad grace.

"What's the matter now?" inquired George as he distributed the canteens among them and placed the coffee-pots beside the fire.

"Come here and see for yourself," replied Loring, taking George by the arm and leading him to the place where the captive Indian lay, all the troopers following at his heels.

"Me good Injun," grunted the prisoner, who seemed to have recovered his senses.

"So I perceive," replied George. "Good Indians steal stock and carry off white boys, don't they?—But I don't see anything about him to laugh at."

"Why, he's nothing but a kid," exclaimed Phillips, "and yet Carey and Loring are both willing to confess that it was all they could do to handle him. They told us a wonderful story about the terrible fight they had before they could tie him, and so we took a look at him, expecting to find him a giant; but instead of that—Well, you can see that he's only a papoose."

George looked down at the boyish face and slender figure of the young warrior, then at the two grizzly old veterans who had fought so hard to capture him, and felt more than half inclined to laugh himself. Either one of them could have strangled him with a finger and a thumb if he could have got hold of him; but getting a good hold was the trouble. An Indian makes up in suppleness and activity what he lacks in strength, and it takes a good man to handle one. Of course the troopers were sorry for their wounded comrade, but they had "got a joke" on him, and it was a long time before he heard the last of it.

The men who had been left to take care of the horses arrived in about an hour, and then George had another disagreeable task to perform, which was to pilot the animals down to the water and find a feeding-ground for them. Being entirely unacquainted with the gully and surrounding country, it took him a long time to do this; but he accomplished it at last, in spite of the darkness, and about one o'clock in the morning he was at liberty to go to his blanket.

The troopers slept later than usual the next morning, for they were all tired out; but Bob's loud call of "Catch up!" brought them to their feet before the sun had risen high enough to send any of his rays into the camp. As there was a good deal to be done and but little time to do it in, four details were made, and certain duties assigned to each. The first, which consisted solely of Loring, was ordered to dish up a cup of coffee in a little less than no time; George and Phillips were instructed to follow up the trail of the missing Indian and see where it led to; Bob and a companion bent their steps toward the sandhill to ascertain the whereabouts of the main body of the expedition; and the others brought in the horses and gave them the grain that was left in the saddle-pockets.

Before ascending the hill Bob and his companion gathered each an armful of dry grass and weeds. These were deposited upon the highest part of the hill and lighted by a match which Bob struck on his coat-sleeve. As soon as the blaze was fairly started, but before the whole pile was ignited, Bob smothered it by throwing on more grass and weeds; and when this was done a column of smoke that could be seen at the distance of fifty miles began to rise in the air.

"Now let me see," said Bob, pulling out the paper which Captain Clinton had copied from his note-book when he started him on the trail. "I want to say, 'Where are you, captain?' and how shall I say it?"

He ran his eye down the page and finally found these instructions:

"A detached party desiring to ascertain the position of the main body will signal as follows: A long smoke of a minute's duration; three short smokes, followed by half a minute's interval; two short smokes, with half a minute's interval; one short smoke, followed immediately by a long one. If the signal is observed, the reply will be the same. If no reply is received in five minutes, repeat from some other and, if possible, higher point, and so continue until an answering signal is seen."

As the reader may not quite understand this, we will tell just how Bob made the signal. He allowed the column of smoke to ascend just one minute by his watch, then took a blanket from his shoulder and with a quick movement threw it over the smoldering pile, holding two of the corners tight to the ground, while his companion held the opposite corners. This, of course, confined the smoke so that no more arose. At the end of half a minute he raised the blanket three times in quick succession, and three balloon-shaped clouds floated off over the sandhills. Waiting half a minute, he lifted the blanket twice, and two more little clouds arose. At the end of another half a minute he permitted a single cloud to escape, and then threw the blanket off altogether; whereupon a long, slender column, like the one that arose when the fire was first started, shot up into the air. Then Bob seated himself on the ground and waited rather anxiously for a reply; but he was not obliged to wait long. Before the five minutes had elapsed an answering smoke was seen; and though it was a long distance off, the atmosphere was so clear, and the white clouds showed so plainly against the blue sky, that the signal could be plainly read. It was the same as the one Bob had just sent up, and so he knew that it was intended for him.

This mode of signalling, which is usually called "tele-graphing by smokes," is in general use among the Plains Indians, and it was from them that our army-officers serving on the border caught the idea. Of course they have a system of their own, which is very different from that of the Indians. The latter cannot read an army-signal, and neither can the officers, with all their striving and scheming, gain a key that will enable them to read the Indian code. It is as much of a mystery as the manner in which a chief conducts a drill of his warriors or controls them in battle without appearing to hold any communication with them. Both these secrets are closely guarded, the Indians considering that it would be "bad medicine" to reveal them to the white man.

"Did you see the exact spot from which that smoke arose?" Bob asked of his companion.

"Yes," answered the trooper.

"Then fix it in your mind, so that you can point it out to George Ackerman. Now that our work is done we will go back to camp."

Breakfast was soon despatched, and in less than half an hour the squad was again on the move, three of the troopers, in order to accommodate the rescued boys and the Indian captive, being obliged to "carry double." Their route lay along the edge of the bluff, within easy reach of water, only three halts being made—one for dinner, and two for the purpose of sending up signals to Captain Clinton. As his replies, which were promptly made, came from the same place, Bob became satisfied that the captain was waiting for him. Of course this caused much speculation among the troopers. Had the captain given up the pursuit, or had he overtaken and scattered the thieves and recovered Mr. Wentworth's stock? Bob was inclined to hold to the latter opinion.

"The captain is a hard man to get away from when he once makes up his mind for business," said he; "and I just know that he's got those cattle, or the most of them. If he has, Mr. Wentworth is all right, for we have got his boys. If your theory is correct—and I begin to believe it is, for everything else has turned out just as you said it would—Lieutenant Earle will come out at the little end of the horn, won't he?"

"Some officer almost always has to do that," answered George. "But the lieutenant will have some honor reflected upon him, if he doesn't win any for himself, for it was a portion of his own troop, commanded by one of his own non-commissioned officers, who rescued the boys."

About two hours before sunset the troopers began to call one another's attention to the fact that the sandhills, among which they had been marching all day long, were growing less in number and height, and to congratulate themselves on drawing near to their journey's end. An hour later they came to the last hill, and as they were riding by it a sentry who had been stationed there presented himself to their view.

CHAPTER XIV

"THREE CHEERS FOR THE 'BRINDLES'!"

"Hallo, Buel!" exclaimed Bob, recognizing in the sentry one of his own company boys, "you'll let us in, won't you?"

"Well, I *am* beat!" replied the man. "Corporal, you're a brick. Three cheers for the 'Brindles'!"

He stood in the "position of a soldier," with his carbine at a "carry," and spoke in a low tone, for he knew that there were officers with field-glasses not far away, and that he had no business to exchange compliments with anybody after this fashion while he was on post. But when he saw the captive Indian and Mr. Wentworth's boys he could not restrain himself.

"Bob, the boys ought to give you a benefit," he added.

"We've got something to show for this scout, even if we are 'Brindles,' haven't we?" said the corporal, holding himself very stiffly in his saddle and looking straight before him, so as not to 'give the sentry away.' "Have you beaten us any?"

"Not by a great sight."

Harry Castlemon

"What have you done, anyway?"

"We've got the most of the stock back, but nary red. Where's Lieutenant Earle?"

"Haven't seen him," answered Bob.

"We haven't seen him either, nor have we heard from him since that courier arrived."

The troopers now found themselves on the border of a wide plain, whose opposite side was bounded by a long line of willows, which fringed the banks of a water-course. On the edge of the willows were gathered the members of the main body, who, having been apprised by their sentinels of the approach of Bob and his party, had assembled to see them come in. Bob began to grow excited at once. He and his men had performed no ordinary exploit, and so impatient was he to have his success known to his comrades that he could not wait until he reached the camp to tell his story.

"You fellows who carry double, ride out there and square yourselves around, so that they can see that we have not returned empty-handed," commanded Bob, who forthwith proceeded to execute his own order by placing the three men who "carried double" one behind the other, broadside to the camp, so that the officers with their field-glasses could observe that each horse had two riders on his back. "I declare I feel like one of those old Roman conquerors—on a small scale; but in order to carry out the role I ought to make one end of a lariat fast to that Indian's neck and drag him into the camp, oughtn't I? That's the way the Romans used to do with their captives, only they chained them to their chariot-wheels. There you are!—Swing your caps, you kids, and holler, to let your father know you are here."

The boys obeyed with alacrity, swinging their caps around their heads and laughing and shouting by turns, while the two soldiers behind whom they rode raised their own caps on the muzzles of their carbines and joined in with a wild soldier yell. George Ackerman kept watch of the camp through his glass to note the movements of its inmates and make reports of the manner in which this demonstration was received by them.

"There's the captain," said he. "He is coming out in front of the men, in company with some of the officers. Now they are all looking at us through their glasses. Now the captain has taken down his glass and is saying something. Here they come!"

It was evident that the captain had reported the result of his observations, for as George uttered these last words and lowered his glass the men broke into a run and dashed across the plain, raising their charging-yell as they came.

"You fellows who carry double, take the post of honor," commanded Bob; "ride at the head of the squad.—Say, boys," he added, facing about in his saddle and speaking to the men behind him, "look out for Wentworth. There was a look in his eye the last time I saw him that I didn't at all like, and when he finds out that we have captured one of the Indians, he may—"

"There he comes now!" exclaimed one of the troopers.

Bob looked toward the camp, and saw that his man had not been mistaken. Behind the troopers, who were still running forward to meet their returning comrades, but rapidly overhauling them with every jump of his horse, was the father of the rescued boys. He rode without saddle, bridle or hat, his long hair was streaming straight out behind him, he carried in his hand the rifle with which he had done such deadly work while he was defending his home, and he was constantly digging his heels into the sides of his horse, as if he were trying to make him go faster. The man could have but one object in view: that was Bob's opinion, and it must have been Captain Clinton's opinion too, judging by his actions. The latter had raised both hands to his face and stood with his head thrown back, as if he were shouting out some orders; but if he gave any they were drowned in the lusty cheers of the approaching troopers, who ran as if they were engaged in a foot-race.

"That man certainly means mischief," said George.

"I am sure of it," replied the corporal. "But I should act in just the same way if I were in his place. I'd put an end to that Indian in spite of all the soldiers that ever wore the 'honored blue;' but that, I know, would be very wrong, for this red imp is one of the government wards, and nobody must presume to lay an ugly hand on him."

"What would be done with Mr. Wentworth if he should shoot your prisoner?" asked George.

"'What would be done with him?'" repeated Bob, bitterly. "Why, he would be put in arrest before he could say 'Jerusalem!' and the agent of the Kiowas would insist on his being tried for murder, notwithstanding the fact that this same Indian was one of the party that burned Mr. Wentworth's house and carried his children into captivity. Why, George, unless you are posted you have no idea—But I will tell you a short story by and by. Just now I must attend to our friend Mr. Wentworth. Stand by me, for I believe I shall need a helping hand before I get through with him."

While this conversation was going on Bob had kept a

watchful eye upon the movements of Mr. Wentworth, who had by this time passed the troopers and was guiding his horse so as to come up on the left flank of Bob's squad. As soon as the latter became satisfied that this was the man's intention, he rode out of the line and placed himself beside the captive Indian, who was riding on Loring's horse and was by no means an uninterested spectator of what passed before him. He too was keeping his gaze directed toward Mr. Wentworth, whom he doubtless recognized.

"White man very angry—heap mad—as mad, in fact, as a wet hen," said Bob, trying to imitate an Indian's way of talking, but making a sad mess of it in his excitement. "He's mad at you for carrying his boys off, and he's going to shoot you dead—heap dead—as dead as a door-nail; and he'll serve you just right, too."

"I hope he won't miss the red and hit me," said Loring.

"You needn't be afraid of that, for these Texans are all good shots," answered Bob; adding in a lower tone, "I'll just tell you what's a fact, Loring: I wouldn't interfere with him if I could help it."

The young savage understood what Bob said, but not a muscle of his face changed. If he had been an old warrior, he would probably have begun his death-chant; but having performed no deeds of which he could boast, he remained silent and calmly awaited the fate that would have been inevitable had it not been for George Ackerman's skill in horsemanship.

The animal on which Mr. Wentworth was mounted was evidently accustomed to being ridden without a bridle, for his master guided him with the greatest ease. When he had almost reached the squad he suddenly swerved from his course, in obedience to a signal conveyed to him by a quick movement of his rider's body, and galloping swiftly around the head of the line stopped short on the other flank. By this unexpected change of tactics the enraged father had gained a position on the unguarded side of the prisoner, and if he had acted as soon as his horse came to a standstill he would have accomplished his purpose in spite of everything; but he could not resist the temptation to talk for just a moment, and that moment's delay defeated him. Cocking his rifle with great deliberation, he said fiercely,

"You have eaten salt in my house, you have slept by my fire, you have drunk from my spring when you were thirsty, you Indian dog, and now—"

When the man had gone thus far rage choked his utterance, and he could not say another word. He drew his rifle to his shoulder, but the muzzle, instead of covering the head of the Indian, covered the person of George Ackerman, who was coming toward him with all the speed his horse could put forth.

The boy had sprung into life and activity the instant he witnessed Mr. Wentworth's cunning manoeuvre, for he knew what it meant. Giving a pull at his left rein, at the same time touching his horse lightly with the spurs, the animal wheeled like a flash on his hind feet, and, dashing through the line behind Bob Owens (some of the troopers afterward declared that he jumped clear over Bob's horse), brought his rider to the right side of the Indian just in time to intercept the deadly aim. In another second George had seized the rifle with both hands, and a terrific struggle began between him and Mr. Wentworth for the possession of the weapon. In less time than it takes to tell it the man, having no stirrups to support him, was jerked off his horse, and before he could recover himself and plant his feet firmly on the ground the rifle was twisted out of his grasp, and the bullet contained in the chamber was sent whistling harmlessly off over the sandhills.

"No more of that!" exclaimed Bob, who rode up just half a minute too late to be of any assistance. "Keep quiet now, or you'll go back to camp with a guard over you."

"Mr. Wentworth," said George, bending down from his saddle and laying his hand upon the angry man's shoulder, "your good sense must tell you that the corporal can't stand peaceably by and see his prisoner shot. What are you thinking of?"

"Give me that gun," panted Mr. Wentworth, who was white to the lips and trembling in every limb. "I'll—I'll—"

"You'll do nothing but behave yourself," interrupted Bob. "You can't have that rifle again until Captain Clinton says so, for you don't know how to act when you have it in your hands; you point it around too loose and reckless. Haven't you something besides revenge to think of now? Can't you see that we have brought your boys back to you safe and sound?"

The man's face softened at once. Tears came to his eyes, and darting quickly around Bob's horse he ran up to his children, and, pulling them both to the ground at once, folded them in his arms. But we will not say any more about that meeting, will we? The joy of a family reunited under circumstances like these is something too sacred to be intruded upon even by a sympathizing pen, isn't it? Even the troopers, some of whom had witnessed many an affecting scene, could not stand it, but turned away their heads and drew their hands hastily across their eyes, as if to brush away something that seemed to be obscuring their vision. One of them caught Mr. Wentworth's horse, and after the latter had mounted and taken his boys up with him, one in front and the other behind, the squad continued its march toward the camp.

When Bob came to look in front of him, he found that the appearance of things had changed somewhat. The comrades who had started out to meet him were no longer advancing in a compact body. They had halted and drawn themselves up in two parallel lines, facing each other, and leaving room enough between them for Bob and his squad to pass through.

"Hallo!" exclaimed the delighted corporal. "The boys have got up a reception for us, and we must meet it in good shape.—Attention, squad! Draw sabres!—Loring, ride on ahead with Mr. Wentworth.—George, come up on my right."

When these orders were issued the men promptly fell into line, conversation ceased on the instant, tobacco was knocked out of pipes that had but just been filled, carbines were adjusted in soldier-fashion, caps that had been worn with the peak behind were turned right side in front, and twelve bright blades leaped from their scabbards. In this order the successful troopers rode by their comrades, who cheered them loudly, and then fell in behind and followed them into camp, marching in column of fours. Bob at once rode up to Captain Clinton's fire, and dismounted to make his report, which he did in this way:

"I have the honor, sir, to report that we surprised five Indians in camp last night, captured one, killed three and released Mr. Wentworth's boys."

"Good for you, corporal!" exclaimed the captain, his astonishment getting the better of him for the moment. "Anybody hurt on your side?"

"One wounded, sir. Private Carey received a knife-thrust in

the right arm while assisting Private Loring to capture the Indian."

"Very good," said the captain, resuming his official tones and dignity at the same time. "Stake out your horses, and then come back here. I want to hear all the particulars. What was the cause of that disturbance out there on the plain?"

"I was the cause of it, cap, you bet," exclaimed Mr. Wentworth, whose face did not look much as it did when he galloped out to meet Bob and his squad. Then it was disturbed with passion; now it was beaming with joy. "I'd ha' sent that Injin to the happy land o' Canaan in a little less than the shake of a buck's tail if Ackerman hadn't stopped me, you bet."

"It was a good thing for you that he did stop you," said the captain quietly. "You would have brought yourself into serious trouble by such a proceeding."

"I know that," said Mr. Wentworth, "but who cares for trouble when his dander's up? Say, cap, may I have my rifle? Ackerman took it away from me."

"You may have it on condition that you will make no more attempts on the life of this prisoner," replied the captain. "There is a law to deal with such fellows as he is."

"Where in the world is it, I'd like to know?" exclaimed Mr. Wentworth fiercely. "It hasn't got out here to Texas yet. If I had shot him, as I meant to do, you would have had a guard over me in no time; but he came with a band of his friends and set fire to my house, and carried off my little boys, and killed my herdsmen, and drove off my stock; and you, knowing it all, stand here, with your hundred and twenty blue-coats, and tell me that I must not touch him. Your colonel will give him up when his agent makes a demand for him, and he'll go back to his reservation, and the government will feed him on good food and give him good clothes, and some rascally trader will sell him more powder and balls to kill white folks with; but if *I*—Dog-gone my buttons!— Ackerman, give me that rifle."

It was plain that Mr. Wentworth's "dander" was still "up"— 'way up. The listening troopers exchanged glances of approval with one another, and would have cheered him if they had dared. Being a civilian, the man was at liberty to talk pretty much as he pleased; but if one of their own number had made such an exhibition of temper in the presence of an officer, he would have been punished for it.

"We will not discuss that matter," said the captain calmly. "I know my business and attend to it strictly, leaving the agents to look out for their own affairs. They are not responsible to me, or to you either, for the manner in which they do the work entrusted to them."

"All right, cap," said Mr. Wentworth, picking up one of his boys and then lowering him carefully to the ground. "Mum is the word, if you say so. But I haven't heard you tell Ackerman to give me that rifle yet."

"Neither have I heard you make that promise," was the reply.

"Well, I'll make it, but I tell you I hate to, mightily."

The captain smiled, and nodded to George, who rode up and handed over the Winchester.

"She's a good one, cap, and when she speaks she means business—*she* does," said Mr. Wentworth, holding the recovered weapon off at arm's length and gazing at it with admiring eyes. "She is sure death on Kiowas, for she knows I have got something ag'inst them. She rubbed out ten of 'em during the last fight she was in, and she'll spoil the good looks of many more of them before I hand her over to my oldest boy for good.—Put her on your shoulder, Sheldon, and come on."

Lifting his youngest child in his arms, Mr. Wentworth walked away, Sheldon marching proudly by his side with the rifle on his shoulder, and the horse following quietly at his heels. Then Bob and George rode away with the squad, the troopers gradually dispersed, and the captain and his officers went back to the blankets on which they had been dozing away the time while waiting for Corporal Owens.

If it had not been for the fact that he had nearly a thousand head of recaptured stock on his hands, the captain would have set out for the fort at once; but it is almost impossible to drive Texas cattle during the night, for they are about half wild, anyway, and as easily stampeded as a herd of buffaloes. Under favorable circumstances two men who understand their business can take care of a herd of five hundred of them; but this stock which the captain had just recovered from the Indians had grown so unmanageable during the short time they had been in the possession of the raiders, who had pushed them ahead night and day at their greatest speed, that it took thirty well-mounted troopers to keep them within bounds. If they became quieted down during the night, the captain intended to set out for the fort with the main body of his men early the next morning, leaving a few of his troopers to assist Mr. Wentworth to drive the cattle in.

"I say, corporal," exclaimed Carey as Bob led his squad away, "where does Wentworth hang out? What mess does he grub with?"

"I don't know," answered Bob. "I saw him going toward the other end of the camp."

"Now, such work as that won't do," continued Carey. "He'll go up there among those high-toned Grays or Blacks, and they will honey around those boys of his and make much of them, and cut us Brindles completely out of their good graces. They belong to us, and they ought to stay with us; don't you say so?"

Bob replied that he did say so.

"Can't we bring them into our mess?" asked Carey.

"You can try. I'll take care of your horse if you want to make the attempt."

Carey at once dismounted, and started back toward the upper end of the camp, and Bob rode on to find the place where his troop had staked out their horses. While he is looking for it we will explain what the words "Grays," "Blacks" and "Brindles," as used by Private Carey, meant.

One of the first things to be done in a new regiment of cavalry, or in an old one that has just been remounted, is to "color the horses." We mean by this that the animals are divided into lots according to their color, the blacks being placed in one lot, the grays in another, the whites in another, and so on. After these divisions are made there are always some "off" horses, such as roans and browns, which are put into a lot by themselves and called the "brindles." The ranking captain then makes his choice of the colors. For the sake of illustration, we will suppose that he prefers to have his company mounted on black horses. He first takes the finest animal in the lot for his own use, his first lieutenant comes next, the second lieutenant next, the first sergeant next, and so on down through all the sergeants and corporals, each one selecting according to his rank. Then those of the privates who have proved themselves to be the best soldiers are called up one by one, and after they have made their selections the shirks and grumblers, like Bristow and Gus Robbins, have to take those that are left.

The captain who is second in command makes the next choice of colors, and his horses are distributed in the same way. The whites are generally chosen next to the last, not because they are not as good or as handsome as the others, but for the reason that it is harder work for the men to keep them clean, and in action they present conspicuous marks for the rifles of the enemy. "The brindles," the horses of all colors and of no color at all to speak of, are the only ones left, and the lowest company commander must take them because he has no choice. He does not like them, and neither do his men, because the troop that is doomed to ride them cannot make so fine appearance on dress-parade as the others do, and for the reason that the Brindles are the butt of all the jokes that old soldiers can play upon one another. When we have said that we have said a good deal, for if there is any mischief that a lot of veterans will not think of when they have a leisure hour on their hands, we don't know what it is.

When the horses were "colored" at Fort Lamoine the brindles fell to the lot of Lieutenant Earle, as he was the lowest company commander, all the others being captains. This was the troop to which Bob Owens belonged, and, in common with its other members, he had suffered from the practical jokes that had been played upon him by the more fortunate troopers. But of late these jokes were not as frequent as they had formerly been, for the "Brindles" had proved themselves to be the best of soldiers. When their achievements were taken into consideration they led every troop in the garrison. They had gallantly borne their part in every duty they were called on to perform, their non-commissioned officers had invariably been successful when sent out in pursuit of deserters, and now one of them had done something for which the members of his regiment were glad to honor him in the way we have described. During the rest of Bob's life at Fort Lamoine but little was said about the despised Brindles; but if any trooper *did* forget himself and make disparaging remarks concerning them or their "ringed, streaked and striped" horses, some listening Brindle would promptly interrupt him with—

"Look here, Bub, we didn't enlist to show ourselves off on dress-parade. When you Blacks" (or Grays or Chestnuts, as the case might be, the offending trooper being designated by the color of the horses on which his company was mounted) "have followed an Indian trail across the Staked Plains, and been burned up by an August sun, and had your mouths and throats filled so full of sand that you couldn't tell the truth for a whole month, and have surprised a party of hostiles in their camp, and rescued two prisoners alive and unharmed,— when you have done all that, you can talk; until then hold your yawp. That feat has never been accomplished but once in the Department of Texas, and then it was accomplished by *our* boys, the Brindles of the—th Cavalry."

Bob and his men were proud of that exploit, and, what was more, they did not mean to be robbed of any of the honor they had won. That was one reason why they wanted to bring Mr. Wentworth and his boys into their mess. They supposed they were going back to the fort with Captain Clinton's command, and they wanted to carry those boys through the gate themselves. But, as it happened, the captain had decided upon something else, and by that decision had unconsciously given Bob's lucky squad of Brindles an opportunity to add to their laurels. We shall see what use they made of it.

CHAPTER XV

MORE BAD LUCK FOR MR. WENTWORTH

While Bob and his men were staking out their horses they were besieged by anxious Brindles who wanted to know just where they had been and what they had done during their absence. No incident connected with the experience of their successful comrades was deemed too trivial for their notice. Bob and the rest answered their questions as fast as they were able, and asked a good many in return. They learned that Captain Clinton had fallen in with the stolen cattle about one o'clock that morning, but the Indians they had hoped to find with them were not to be seen. The captain had pursued them so closely that they did not have time to drive the stock into the Staked Plains, to die there of thirst, and neither did they harass the column, as George said they would. Their force was too small to accomplish anything by it. The captain had spent all the forenoon in gathering up the stock, and it was now feeding on the prairie close by, guarded by a large squad of troopers.

"I'll tell you what's a fact, boys," said one of the Brindles. "This raid must have been a big thing, for just after you left us we struck the trail of a large drove that joined ours, and a little farther on we found another. But they were both older than our own, so the scout said, and the drove we followed was left behind as a sort of bait for us to swallow, while the main herd was driven off."

"Why didn't you go on after the main herd?" asked Bob.

"It would have been of no use. It had too much of a start; and besides, we have already got just as much on our hands as we can attend to. We have been all day gathering up the cattle we have got, and it is just all we can do to hold fast to them. The fellows up there must attend to the rest."

By "the fellows up there" the troopers meant to indicate the cavalry attached to the several posts north of the Staked Plains.

When Bob went back to the captain's head-quarters, George, being a privileged character, went with him. The officer questioned them closely in regard to their movements, took copious notes to assist him in making out his report to the colonel, and by the time he got through he came to the conclusion that the two young men deserved especial mention for the skill and courage they had exhibited. He rewarded them on the spot by giving them more work to do—some that was not supposed to have any danger in it, but which, nevertheless, gave them an opportunity to show whether the success that had attended them during their last scout was owing to good luck or good management.

"I am more than satisfied, because you have accomplished more than I expected of you," said the captain as he put his note-book into his pocket. "As you will probably have some hard riding to do to-morrow, I will see that you are allowed a good night's rest."

"Are we going back to the fort in the morning, sir?" asked George.

Although Bob was fully as anxious as his companion was to know what the captain meant by saying that he and his squad would probably have some hard riding to do the next day, he never would have dared to ask such a question; and if he had, the officer, if he had made any reply at all, would very likely have told him that he would find out all about it in due time. But he expressed no surprise at George's inquisitiveness.

"*I* am going back to fort," said he, "but you and the corporal will have to stay and help Mr. Wentworth with the cattle. You will be of more use to him, George, than half a dozen green hands, for you know how to drive stock and can act as instructor to the rest. You know where Holmes's ranche is, I suppose? Well, I shall want the corporal to stay with Mr. Wentworth until he gets there, and then you will have to guide the squad to the fort. If you should happen to meet any raiders on the way, why take them in," added the captain with a smile.—"Corporal, is Carey badly hurt?"

"He grumbles a good deal, sir, but I think it is more from anger than pain."

"Perhaps you had better take a man in his place and let him go to the fort with us, so that the doctor can look at his arm," said the captain.

"I tell you there is nothing like having friends at court," said Bob as he and George walked away. "Until you came among us I didn't know that these officers could be so very friendly and good-natured. Why, George, if I knew the country as well as you do, and could get scout's pay, I would stay in the army all my life. We have got a sort of roving commission now, and I hope we can do something with it before we go back to the fort."

Details for such duties as this which had just been assigned to Corporal Owens are about the only recreations that fall to the lot of a private soldier on the Plains, and they are eagerly sought after. Being almost always commanded by a sergeant or corporal who has proved to the satisfaction of his superiors that he can be trusted, the men never fail to enjoy themselves to the fullest extent. It is a great relief to them to be entirely out of reach of their Argus-eyed officers, who are so prompt to take them to task for the least neglect of duty.

When they reached the place where the Brindles were encamped, they found that Carey had been successful in his mission. He had brought Mr. Wentworth and his boys back with him, and the troopers were crowded about them listening to Sheldon's account of his experience among the Kiowas.

"Get all you can out of them, boys," exclaimed Bob, "for you will not see them after to-night."

"Why won't we?" asked half a dozen troopers at once.

"Because they are not going to the fort. They are going to Holmes's ranche, wherever that is, and we're going to see them safely there with the stock."

"We? who?"

"Our same old squad—all except Carey."

The owner of that name, whose face had lighted up with pleasure, jumped to his feet with an angry exclamation. "What do you mean by that, corporal?" he demanded.

"It's no fault of mine, Carey," replied Bob. "The captain thinks you had better go to the fort, so that the doctor can look at your wound."

Carey made no reply, but elbowed his way through the crowd and started toward the other end of the camp. In a few minutes he was standing in front of Captain Clinton with his hand to his cap.

"What is it, Carey?" asked that officer after he had returned the salute.

"My respects to you, sir," answered the trooper, "and, if I might take the liberty, I'd like to know why I am to be left behind while the rest of our squad goes off on a picnic with them cattle?"

"Why, you are wounded," said the captain.

"Just a little scratch, sir," protested the trooper. "But even if I had no right arm at all, I could ride and shoot, and when it came to yelling I'd be there too."

"Very good. If you think you can stand it, go on."

"Thank you, sir. I knew you wouldn't go back on old Carey. I've been in every muss my troop has been in, and nobody ever hinted that I didn't do my duty."

The captain nodded his head and waved his hand in token of dismissal, and the trooper hurried away.

Up to this time George Ackerman had always messed with the officers, but that night he took supper with Bob's squad, because both he and they considered that he belonged to it. During the progress of the meal he reminded the corporal that the latter had promised to tell him a story.

"Oh yes," said Bob, after thinking a moment. "I was telling you, I believe, that if Mr. Wentworth killed that Indian he would be arrested and tried for murder. Well, that's an Indian's idea of justice, and it seems to be the agents' idea too. The Indians think they have a perfect right to kill and scalp whenever they feel like it, but if a white man kills one of them it is an awful thing. If they can't get hold of the man who did the shooting or any of his relations, they look to the government for pay. On a certain occasion a scouting-party of ten men was surprised and utterly wiped out. The surprise was so complete that every one of the party was killed at the first fire, with the exception of a corporal, who had just time to knock over two of the reds before he too was shot. Shortly afterward a peace was patched up, and a band of braves came in, bringing with them an old woman for whom they asked a government pension because her two sons had fallen in battle. Inquiries were made, and it turned out that these two sons were the very Indians who had been killed by the corporal. What do you think of such impudence?"

George did not know what to think of it, and probably the reader doesn't either; but this very incident is on record.

By daylight the next morning the camp was deserted. The main body of the troops was riding rapidly toward Fort Lamoine, and a few miles behind it came the herd which Captain Clinton had recaptured. It was moving leisurely along in front of Mr. Wentworth and George, who controlled it with less difficulty than the rest of the squad would have experienced in managing a dozen cattle. Behind them came Bob and his men, with the two boys, who were mounted on a couple of their father's horses which had been found with the herd. George's quick eye had already noticed that there were at least half a dozen different brands among the cattle, and he told himself that when the animals bearing these brands had been delivered up to their lawful owners, Mr. Wentworth would have very little stock left.

Bob and his troopers enjoyed this "picnic" by being lazy. They had nothing to do worth speaking of but to follow along in the rear of the herd and talk to the boys, the most of the work being performed by George and Mr. Wentworth, who during the first part of the journey managed the cattle both day and night. They offered to assist in any way they could, but the practised herders did not need them, and besides, they were afraid to trust them.

"I don't want to lose these steers and horses again, after all the trouble I have had to get them," Mr. Wentworth always replied. "I know you are good soldiers, or else you couldn't have got my boys back for me; but you can't herd cattle. The least awkward movement on your part would send them galloping back toward the Staked Plains again. Wait until they get over their fright, and then you can try your hands at guarding them during the night."

On the afternoon of the fifth day Bob noticed that George's field-glass was often brought into requisition both by himself and Mr. Wentworth, and on riding forward to inquire the cause of it, he was informed that they were looking for Mr. Taylor's ranche.

"And who is Mr. Taylor?" was Bob's next question.

"He is one of Mr. Wentworth's neighbors who was raided by the Indians. We know it, for we have some of his cattle with us; but whether or not they did him any damage beyond stealing his stock, we don't know; and we can't tell, either, until we find his house if it is still standing, or the ruins of it if it has been destroyed."

"Then we must be getting pretty near our journey's end," said Bob, whose arms and shoulders began to ache when he thought of the tedious routine of drill and guard-duty upon which he must enter as soon as he returned to the fort.

"I don't know what you mean by *near*," replied George. "The fort is all of a hundred and fifty miles from here, and we are not going toward it. We are going toward Holmes's ranche; and even if we have the best of luck, it will take us two weeks to get there."

"That sounds better," said Bob, who was greatly relieved. "When you spoke of Mr. Wentworth's neighbors, I was afraid that our pleasure-excursion was about to be brought to an end, for he doesn't live so *very* far from the fort, you know."

"It's just over there," shouted Mr. Wentworth at this moment. "I see cattle, and that proves that the raiders didn't scoop Taylor as they did me. Now look sharp; we've got rounding out enough to do already."

"What does he mean by that?" asked Bob.

"He means that we mustn't allow our cattle to mix in with Mr. Taylor's, for if we do we shall have to round them all out again. By 'rounding out' we mean separating the different herds from each other; and that is something that none but good herdsmen can do. It requires skill and a big stock of patience, I tell you. Just let a few green hands try it, and see how much they would make at it. Why, they would scare the cattle so that they would run clear out of the State."

Although Mr. Wentworth had declared that Mr. Taylor's ranche was "just over there," our friends did not reach it that day, nor until late in the afternoon of the next. Before they got there they knew just what Mr. Taylor's experience with the Kiowa raiders had been, for they had passed two or three of his herds, whose keepers had told them all about it. The

Indians had suddenly made their appearance, coming from the south, and driving before them a large number of cattle; and although they had not come within five miles of Mr. Taylor's ranche, they had picked up one of his small herds which happened to be in their path.

Our friends camped that night close by Mr. Taylor's ranche, which proved to be a perfect little fort. It was built of heavy stone, was well supplied with provisions, and defended by five stalwart fellows who were armed with Winchester rifles. The raiders would have had a nice time of it if they had come there. The owner listened in great surprise to Mr. Wentworth's story, made much of his boys, and would not let him and George "round out" the stock that bore his brand.

"You're welcome to the steers, neighbor," said he. "I've got more left than I can take care of if the Kiowas bounce me as earnestly as they did you, and you will need them to help you start a new herd."

This same thing was repeated by every one of the half a dozen other ranchemen to whom Mr. Wentworth offered to surrender their stock. They all sympathized with him, and wanted to aid him by every means in their power. The result was, that our friends arrived within one day's march of their journey's end with just as many cattle as they had when they left the Staked Plains. Although Mr. Wentworth had been "completely cleaned out," he was still worth something like twenty thousand dollars.

George and his party made their last camp a short distance from the cabin of a squatter, who rode over to see them during the evening. He went home about ten o'clock, and George and his companions lay down on their blankets, leaving the herd to the care of four mounted troopers. The latter, who during the journey had exhibited the greatest eagerness to learn something of the mysteries of cattle-herding, had so far progressed in knowledge and skill as to be able to stand guard at night, and to give George and Mr. Wentworth an opportunity to obtain the rest of which they began to stand so much in need. About midnight George mounted his horse and rode around the herd to assure himself that everything was just as it should be. He went on horseback, because everybody rides while working about Texas cattle. If a man should venture among them on foot during the daytime, his life would be in danger; and if he went around them at night, he would probably stampede the whole herd.

"All serene," said Loring, who was the first guard George encountered during his rounds. "The moon shines so brightly that I can see the movements of every steer in the drove."

"If we were a little nearer the river perhaps things wouldn't be quite so serene," answered George. "The Mexicans take just such a night as this for their raids."

About an hour after George had retired to his blanket Loring noticed that the cattle began to show signs of uneasiness. Those that were standing up began to move about, those that were lying down arose and moved about with them, and presently the whole herd was in motion. The cattle did not attempt to run away, but walked restlessly about, as if they were unable to find a place that suited them.

"Suke, thing! suke, thing!" said Loring coaxingly.

The travelled reader would have said at once that Loring was a Southerner; and if he could have heard Phillips on the other side of the cattle trying to soothe them with "Co-boss! co-boss!" he would have said that Phillips was from the North. But the cattle did not understand either of them, or if they did they paid no attention to them. Their restlessness increased every moment, and finally Loring, good soldier though he was, deserted his post and started for camp as fast as he could make his horse walk.

"Ackerman," said he in an excited voice, "get up. There is something wrong with those cattle."

George was on his feet in an instant. One glance at the herd was enough.

"I should say there was something wrong!" he exclaimed. "How long has this thing been going on?"

"Not more than five minutes."

"Which way are they looking," continued George.

"Every way, but the most of them keep their heads in that direction," said Loring, waving his arm toward the south.

"Call everybody in camp while I speak to Bob and Mr. Wentworth. No noise now. I am afraid we are going to have trouble."

In less than two minutes all the troopers had been aroused, and George was holding an earnest consultation with Mr. Wentworth and the corporal. "I've seen cattle act that way before," said he, speaking as rapidly as he could make his tongue move, for time was precious; "and if we were a little nearer the river I could easily tell what is the matter with them; but I never heard of the Greasers coming so far into the country as this, and it may be nothing but nervousness that's troubling them. My advice would be to mount the men and move them quietly in line on the north side of the herd, and perhaps by making such a show of numbers we can keep them within bounds until they are quieted down.—What do you say, Mr. Wentworth?"

"It is the only thing that can be done," replied Mr. Wentworth, who seemed to be greatly excited and alarmed; "and even that is a slim chance.—Make haste, corporal. Do all you can for me, for if I lose this herd I shall be ruined, sure enough."

"Catch up!" commanded Bob.

"Look here," said George, seizing his friend by the shoulder and speaking with all the earnestness he could throw into his tones: "if you get in line in front of those cattle, and they start to run toward you, don't try to stop them, for you can't do it, any more than we could stop those buffaloes the other night. Run before them, and gradually draw off to the right or left of them, and you will get safely off; otherwise they will certainly run over you. But I am afraid it is too late to do anything," added George as he noted the increasing restlessness of the cattle.

"It is too late! it is too late!" exclaimed Mr. Wentworth, rubbing his hands nervously together. "There they go!"

Even as he spoke a noise like the rumbling of distant thunder sounded in their ears, and instantly the whole herd made off at the top of its speed. Looking over the mass of horns and tails that was tossed wildly in the air, the troopers were horrified to see Phillips standing directly in front of it. Being fully determined to do his duty to the utmost, the brave fellow sat in his saddle, swinging his arms about his head, and no doubt shouting at the top of his voice to stop the advance of the frightened herd, which was bearing down upon him with the resistless power of an avalanche.

"The man is crazy!" cried George in great alarm. Then, raising both hands to his face and using them as a speaking-trumpet, he yelled, with all the power of his lungs,

"Run! run for your life!"

Phillips afterward said that he did not hear what George said to him—in fact, he couldn't hear anything but the noise of those hoofs—but, seeing that if he remained where he was his death was certain, he wheeled his horse and fled with the speed of the wind. The last his friends saw of him was as he dashed over the top of a ridge, with the stampeded cattle close behind him. When they were all out of sight and the rumble of their hoofs had died away in the distance, the troopers turned to look at Mr. Wentworth. He stood with his hands in his pockets gazing disconsolately in the direction in which the herd had disappeared, but had nothing to say.

"Now, here's a go!" whispered Bob, giving George a nudge in the ribs with his elbow. "What am I to do? This is something Captain Clinton didn't think to provide for, isn't it? I was ordered to go to Holmes's ranche with Mr. Wentworth, but I wasn't told to follow up and collect his cattle if they were stampeded."

"You mustn't think of following them up," said George decidedly. "There is no man in the world who could get that same herd together again, for it will join others as soon as it gets over its fright; and how could we tell these cattle from others bearing the same brand? They are gone, and that's all there is of it. You must mount at once and see if you can find anything of Phillips."

"All right!—Mr. Wentworth," said Bob, "we are very sorry for the loss you have sustained, but we have done all we could for you."

"I know it, corporal, and I am very grateful to you and to the captain, who was kind enough to send you with me. Such things as these will happen sometimes, in spite of everything. Now I hardly know what to do."

Neither would anybody else have known what to do under the same circumstances. Mr. Wentworth had no home, no property except his rifle and the horses he and his boys rode, no work to do, and but little to eat in his haversack. It was a trying situation for a man who but a few days before had been worth a fortune, and almost any one would have been disheartened.

"I'll tell you what you can do," said George. "You can easily find your way to the Ackerman settlement, and if you go there and give Mr. Gilbert a note of introduction which I will write for you, he will take care of you until you can decide upon something."

George did not feel at liberty to tell Mr. Wentworth all he had on his mind. As soon as he returned to the fort he intended to write to his guardian, asking him if he might furnish Mr. Wentworth with a sufficient number of cattle from his own herds to give the impoverished man a new start in life. Of course Mr. Wentworth had a few cattle of his own among those that had just run off, but it would take some time to gather them up; and as he would not want to be troubled with his boys while he was engaged in the work, George intended to ask Mr. Gilbert to take care of them during their father's absence, and to lend Mr. Wentworth a few good herdsmen to assist him in getting his stock together. While he was thinking about it, and before Mr. Wentworth could thank him for his generous offer, something happened which told them very plainly that the stampede that had just taken place was not owing to the nervousness of the cattle, but to the presence of those of whom George Ackerman had every reason to stand in fear.

Their attention was first attracted by some unusual sound. They could not have told what it was or from which direction it came, but they all heard it, and waited for it to be repeated, that they might locate and define it. There was a moment's silence, and then a chorus of wild yells arose on the night air, accompanied by the rapid discharge of firearms. The troopers looked at one another in blank amazement, and then at George, who was not long in assigning a cause for the disturbance.

"The Greasers are attacking the squatter," he exclaimed; and he was quite as much astonished to be called upon to say it as the troopers were to hear it. It must be a strong and daring band that would venture so far into the country, and almost involuntarily George whispered the name of Fletcher. Bob was quick to decide upon his course. He knew just what Captain Clinton would expect of him if he were there.

"Mr. Wentworth," said he, "we must lend that man a helping hand. As you can't go with us on account of your boys, you will have to look out for yourself and them."

"And I am just the man who can do it," replied Mr. Wentworth. "Good-bye and good luck to you! Shoot hard, and shoot to hit."

"How cool and confident he is! I wish I had half his courage," thought Bob as he ordered his men into their saddles, following it up with the commands, "Forward! Trot! gallop!"

The troopers fell into line as they moved off, and a few yards in advance of them rode George and Bob. The former could easily have taken the lead if he had desired to do so, but, knowing that he did not command the squad, he curbed his impatience as well as he could and kept close by his friend's side. The troopers unslung their carbines, George made ready his Winchester, while Bob, who believed as firmly in the virtues of "cold steel" as did the gallant officer whom he afterward accompanied on his last memorable march, drew his sabre. All on a sudden the firing ceased, and when the troopers rode over the brow of a ridge a few minutes later, they saw a thin blue smoke arising from the squatter's cabin, and that told them more than they wanted to know. George was both astonished and enraged at the sight—astonished to know that the raiders would stop during one of their marauding expeditions, when haste was so necessary, to attack and burn so humble a dwelling as the abode of the squatter, and enraged to see that they had been successful enough to do even that. There was a crowd of Mexicans around the building, and others with horses were standing close by.

"Gobble the horses, Bob," said George, who was so highly excited that he could scarcely speak, "and then you can ride down and capture the raiders at your leisure."

Bob caught the idea in an instant. Turning in his saddle, he waved his sabre over his head, but instead of giving the command "Charge!" he effectually closed the mouths of his followers, who had already opened their lips and drawn in a long breath preparatory to giving vent to their favorite yell, by saying in a low tone, "Silence!"

Bob did not know whether or not this order had ever before been given during a charge, and, what was more, he did not care. His object was to cut the men who were lingering about the burning cabin off from their horses, and in order to do that he must get as close as he could to them before he was discovered.

CHAPTER XVI

CONCLUSION

The men about the cabin were so engrossed in their work of destruction, and the horse-guards were so intent on watching them, that Bob's advance was not discovered until he and his followers were within less than two hundred yards of the cabin. So entirely unexpected was their appearance that for a moment the cattle-thieves were struck motionless with astonishment; then they recovered their power of action, and those who were on foot made a rush for their horses. Some succeeded in reaching them, but others did not. Two or three of them fell before the carbines of the troopers, who opened a hot fire as soon as they saw that they were discovered, and the horse-guards, believing that the attacking party was backed up by a large force of soldiers which was close at hand, instantly put spurs to their nags and galloped off, taking the loose horses with them and leaving their companions to look out for themselves.

"Throw down and throw up, Greasers!" commanded Corporal Owens as he dashed up to the cabin swinging his sabre over his head; and the order, which meant, "Throw down your weapons and throw up your hands," was obeyed by five sullen fellows, who muttered Spanish oaths between their teeth and looked mad enough to do almost anything.

Harry Castlemon

There was no fight at all. If there had been a shot fired at the troopers, they didn't know it. The party that had gone off with the horses outnumbered Bob's, and could, beyond a doubt, have driven them off the field if they had only thought so; but their surprise was complete, and, more than that, they were demoralized. The presence of the troopers they regarded as part of a pre-concerted plan to cut them off from the river, and that frightened them more than Bob's sudden onslaught.

"Still another feather for your cap, Corporal Owens," said George, after he and Loring and a few others had taken a shot or two apiece at the retreating cattle-thieves, "and nobody hurt on our side, either. Now I—What are you doing here? Is this the way you keep your promise?"

These questions were addressed to one of the prisoners, who took off his sombrero and scratched his head as if he were trying to stir up his ideas so that he could make some reply to these peremptory interrogations.

"Springer," continued George, slowly, "what are you doing here? Where's the squatter?"

"In there," replied the cattle-thief, jerking his head toward the cabin, which was now fairly ablaze and sending out so much heat that the troopers were obliged to draw away from it. "He never would have touched him, Fletcher wouldn't, if he had kept in the house an' left us alone; but he plumped one of us over when we fust came up; an' this here is the consequence," added Springer, nodding his head toward the cabin again.

George knew why it was that the cattle-thieves had stopped to destroy the squatter's house. He had killed one of their number, and they, in turn, had killed him after a hard fight, and it was now too late to recover his body or to save a single thing the cabin contained.

"So this is the fellow who twice befriended you, is it?" said Bob, who was surprised to hear George call one of the prisoners by name. "Don't you think it would be a good plan to chuck him into the fire too?"

"*I* do," said Loring fiercely.

Springer drew a little nearer to George for protection.

"I didn't have any hand in it," said he earnestly—"honor bright, I didn't. I can explain everything, so that you can see that I am not to blame for being here."

"Carey," exclaimed Bob, "go back to Mr. Wentworth and give him his choice between taking care of himself and going to the fort with us. Hurry up, now.—If I only had a spade or two, I would make these prisoners bury their dead comrades."

"Springer," said George, "can these friends of yours understand English?"

The cattle-thief replied that they could not; they were all Mexicans.

"I am glad to hear it, for I want to ask you a few questions before you explain how you came to be here. Did Fletcher have his whole band with him to-night?"

"Not half of 'em," was the reply; "he had only about thirty men."

"How many has he in all?"

"Two hundred or so."

"Does he still make his head-quarters at the Don's ranche?"

"Yes; but look here, Mr. George," said Springer earnestly; "if you are goin' over there after him, be mighty careful. You know what sort of a looking place that ranche is—all stone, you know—an' them fellows is all old soldiers, an' they'll fight awful."

George nodded his head as if to say that he knew all about that, and spent some minutes in questioning the prisoner in regard to the road that led to the ranche, while Bob sat by on his horse and listened. By the time George had heard all he wanted to know, and Springer had told how he had been arrested by the officer at Eagle Pass and rescued by Fletcher, Carey came back.

"Mr. Wentworth will take care of himself," reported the trooper. "He says that if he went to the fort he would have to come back to Holmes's ranche, anyway—he is going to make his home there for a while, for he and Holmes were boys together—and so he might just as well go there in the first place, and save time and travelling. He sent his best wishes to everybody, and hopes we will catch all the scoundrels who wiped out the squatter."

"I wish we could," said Bob, facing about in his saddle and gazing in the direction in which the thieves had retreated; "but we have five prisoners to take care of, and so our hands are tied."

"You just ought to have seen him, corporal," continued Carey. "He had thrown his three horses in a sort of triangle by tying their feet together and tripping them up in some way, and there he lay with his boys behind his living breastworks, all ready for a fight. Grit to the last, wasn't he? When I asked him why he hadn't mounted and dug out as soon as we left, he said that that wouldn't have been safe, for he might have run right in among the Greasers before he knew it."

"Well, boys," said Bob, gazing sorrowfully at the glowing bed of coals that covered the site of the squatter's cabin, "there is nothing more we can do here, and so we will make a break for the fort."

"Look here, corporal," said one of the troopers: "if you are going to make us carry double with those dirty Greasers, I am going to kick."

"Don't you worry," answered Bob. "I shouldn't do it myself, and of course I sha'n't ask you to do it. They'll have to walk.—Springer, draw these Mexican gentlemen up in line."

Springer gave the necessary order in Spanish, and it was sullenly obeyed.

"Just remind them, Springer, that if they don't step faster than that somebody may hasten their movements with a prod from the point of a sabre," said Bob angrily. "We are in no humor to stand a great deal of nonsense from them. Now, right-face them; that's better.—Fall in around them, squad, four on each flank and four in the rear. Forward, march!—Now, George, which way is the fort from here?"

"Off there," replied George, "but I am going to take you to the river-trail."

"What for?"

"So that you can get something to eat."

If they had been a little farther down the river, say about twenty-five miles, George would have taken them to his own house. It would have given him no little pleasure to entertain these companions of a long, toilsome and dangerous scout under his own roof; but of course he could not think of leading them out of their way in order to do it. They found plenty to eat after they reached the river-trail, but the ranchemen at whose houses they halted could give them no information concerning the raiders. They had been on that side of the river, and had gone back empty-handed, and that was all the ranchemen knew about the matter. This made it plain that Bob's gallant dash had not been without its effect. It had frightened the thieves so thoroughly that they dared not stop to pick up any of the cattle they found in their way.

Bob and his troopers camped that night near a farm-house whose owner was so delighted to see the five prisoners they had brought with them, and to learn of the success that had attended them ever since Captain Clinton sent them off by themselves, that he insisted on giving them a seat at his table. The next morning he gave them a breakfast; but the first squad who went in—which included Bob and George—had scarcely taken possession of their chairs when one of the sentries was heard calling lustily for the corporal of the guard. Bob excused himself and ran out, only to return again almost immediately and startle everybody with the order, "Boots and saddles!" George jumped up from the table, wondering what was the matter. When he reached the porch he found out. About a mile up the trail was a long column of blue-coats coming down at a sweeping trot.

"They are our boys, and they are after the Greasers," exclaimed Bob, as George came down the steps. "It's lucky we are here, for you are the very man they want if they are going across the river.—Catch up, boys, and fall in just as we do when we are on the march, only face to the left, so as to front the column when it comes up."

If we have a reader who is familiar with cavalry tactics, he will have discovered, long before this time, that Corporal Owens was not at all particular as to the orders he gave, provided he could make his men act to suit him. When in the presence of his superiors he always gave the proper commands, in order to save himself from the reproof that would have promptly followed the slightest departure from the tactics; but when he was in command of a scouting-party he was decidedly free and easy. Even an old trooper might have been puzzled over this last order, but the men who had marched with him so many miles were quick to catch his meaning and prompt to carry out his wishes; so that when the whole available cavalry force of Fort Lamoine, numbering two hundred men, came sweeping by the farm-house a few minutes later, with Captain Clinton riding at the head, they were astonished to see Bob's little squad drawn up in a hollow square, with their prisoners in the centre. Of late there had been a good many anxious inquiries made concerning these very men, and here they were, safe and sound, and, wonderful to tell, with more prisoners to show what good soldiers they were.

"Three cheers for the 'Brindles,' the old reliables!" shouted the sergeant-major; and the yells that arose from two hundred pairs of strong lungs could have been heard a long distance away.

George lifted his cap in response to a nod of recognition from Captain Clinton, and in obedience to a sign from him rode over to his side; but Bob and his men sat in their saddles as stiff as so many posts, looking straight to the front. When the next call for cheers came, however, it almost knocked Bob over.

"Three cheers for Sergeant Owens!" shouted a "Brindle;" and then came three more yells, followed by a "tiger" as loud and piercing as an Indian war-whoop. During his absence Bob had been promoted in general orders for gallantry, his pay as sergeant to begin on the day he rescued Mr. Wentworth's boys from the hands of the Kiowas.

Presently the bugle sounded, and the column came to a halt. The officers at once fell out and crowded around George, who, in as few words as possible, told Captain Clinton what Bob's squad had been doing since the captain left them back there on the borders of the Staked Plains. The officers were all very much pleased, especially Lieutenant Earle, who for a moment threw off his dignity and rode up to thank the members of the squad which had brought so much credit upon the troop he commanded.

"Sergeant," said he, extending his hand—which Bob accepted after running his own hand through his sword-knot and dropping his sabre by his side—"I congratulate you and all your men. You have done well."

Bob managed to stammer out something about being glad to have pleased the lieutenant, and the latter, after ordering them to sheathe their sabres, went on to tell how he had followed the Indians in his front until his men and horses were nearly exhausted and almost dead for want of water, and how he had finally returned to the fort a day behind the column, utterly disgusted with his want of success, to find that some of his own troop had carried off the honors of the scout. He was proud to command such men.

Meanwhile, Captain Clinton and George were engaged in an earnest consultation. The former told the young scout that he been sent out to punish the raiders who had just recrossed the river, and that he was going to do it, too. He was going to drive them out of their stronghold, and George must show him the way to it. His men had already had their coffee, but as George and the rest of Bob's squad had had none, they might stay there at the farm-house until they had eaten the breakfast that had been prepared for them, and then ride on rapidly and overtake the column, which would move down the trail at a trot. This having been decided upon, a squad was made up of details from the different companies to take charge of the prisoners, and the command given to a corporal, who was instructed to take them to the fort. Then the column rode on, the corporal marched off with his captives, and Bob and his troopers went back to the farm-house to eat their breakfast.

During the meal George Ackerman, who had thus far been one of the gayest of the party, was very silent and thoughtful. It was almost impossible for any one to get a word out of him. His face was as white as a sheet, but although everybody noticed it, Bob Owens was the only one who could account for it. When they had satisfied their appetites they went out to hold the horses, so that the rest of the squad could come in, and George and the new sergeant, who was not a little elated over his unexpected promotion, led their nags off on one side, so that they could converse without being overheard.

"I know just how it is," said Bob, "for I have felt so ever since Captain Clinton ordered me to follow up that trail. When you know that a good many lives besides your own depend upon a decision you may have to make in an instant of time, I tell you it is rather trying to a fellow's nerves. I used to envy the colonel and all the other high officers in the garrison, but I wouldn't give up my little sergeant's berth for double the money they make. There's too much responsibility connected with the positions they hold."

George told himself that that was just the objection to his own position. He began to see that being a scout meant something. There were two hundred men in Captain Clinton's command, and what if they should all be sacrificed by some blunder on his part?

As soon as the rest of the troopers had eaten breakfast, and Bob had thanked the farmer for his hospitality, the troopers sprang into their saddles and galloped after the column. When they overtook it George rode up beside the captain, and the Brindles, without creating the least confusion, fell into their usual places—all except Bob Owens, who did not belong in the ranks any longer. Being second sergeant, his place was in the rear of his company, "opposite the left file of the rear four;" and that was the position he fell into as soon as he had reported the arrival of his squad to the lieutenant.

"Well, Ackerman," said Captain Clinton as the boy galloped up beside him, "we are in your hands. We want to go to the nearest ford, and we don't want to get there before dark."

"Very good, sir. If you will move the column in that direction," said George, indicating a 'right oblique,' "you will cut off twenty miles, and besides, you can walk all the way, and save your horses for a rapid eighteen-mile ride that must come as soon as we cross the river."

We need not dwell upon the incidents of that day's march, or enlarge upon the feeling of suspense that George Ackerman experienced during that "rapid eighteen-mile ride" to which he had referred. It will be enough to say that they crossed the ford just after dark in safety; that George, without the least difficulty, found the narrow road that led from the river to Don Miguel's ranche; that at his suggestion the column marched "right by twos," which changed the troopers from four to two abreast, Captain Clinton and George riding at the head; that they moved as silently as possible, so as not to alarm any of the people living along the route, and rapidly, in order to reach the ranche before the cattle-thieves could receive notice of their approach; and that at the end of two hours they galloped into the valley and saw Fletcher's stronghold in plain view before them. A single glance at it showed them that they had arrived just in the nick of time. The courtyard was lighted up with lanterns, excited men were moving to and fro, loud voices were heard shouting out words of command, and the whole interior of the building presented a scene of the wildest commotion. Some watchful friend had got ahead of the column and warned the thieves, and they were gathering up their plunder preparatory to beating a hasty retreat. They were on the watch too, for the column had scarcely made its appearance when a sentry called out, "Who is it?" (equivalent to "Who goes there?"), following up his challenge with the cry of "The Americans! the Americans!"

George afterward said that he never had a very clear idea of what happened during the next few minutes. He remembered that he heard the bugle sound a charge; that he dashed through the arched stone gateway at headlong speed side by side with Captain Clinton; and that the rapid discharge of firearms rang in his ears, accompanied by the cries of the cattle-thieves, who fled in every direction, and such cheers and yells from the troopers as he had never heard before. When he came to himself, his horse, which seemed to enter fully into the spirit of the matter, was dancing about in front of a pile of forage that filled one end of the courtyard. When George saw it he threw himself from his saddle and caught up a lantern.

"I have seen the inside of this hole for the last time," said he to himself. "If Fletcher lives to make a prisoner of me, he shall not bring me to this ranche, and neither shall he harbor here to raid on my stock."

As these thoughts passed through the boy's mind he smashed the glass globe of the lantern with one savage kick, and picking up the lamp applied the flame to the pile of forage. He set it on fire in half a dozen different places, and then turned and threw the lamp into one of the nearest rooms, which seemed to be well filled with something. When he had done that he was frightened. What if it was powder in there? But, fortunately, it wasn't. It was some combustible matter that blazed up fiercely, sending huge volumes of flames out of the door and lighting up the courtyard, which was now occupied only by American troopers. The cattle-thieves had behaved just as they did when Bob Owens so gallantly attacked a portion of their number at the squatter's cabin. They fled in hot haste, making their escape by the roof, by doors whose existence George never dreamed of, and by squeezing themselves through the narrow openings that served the ranche in the place of windows. And, strange to tell, there was no one injured on either side. Having satisfied himself on this point by searching all the rooms to make sure that there were no dead or wounded men in them, the captain ordered his troopers into the saddle and departed as rapidly and silently as he had come. George looked over his shoulder now and then, and when he saw the thick clouds of smoke that arose in the air growing thicker and blacker, he told himself that he had made sure work of the old ranche, and that it would never serve the cattle-thieves for a harboring-place again.

Of course there was an "investigation" made by the Mexican government, but if it ever amounted to anything, George never heard of it. The expedition certainly had a moral effect, and no doubt that was just what the department commander wanted. A body of Mexican troops was ordered to the river almost immediately, and after that the raiders were by no means as bold as they had formerly been. They crossed the Rio Grande now and then lower down, toward Eagle Pass, but the troopers there were on the alert, and after they had thrashed the thieves a few times on their own ground, and some of their leaders had been arrested by the Mexican authorities, the Texans began to feel comparatively safe.

George Ackerman was kept actively employed at the fort much longer than he thought he would be when he first went there. By order of Colonel Brown he crossed the river on several occasions disguised in his Mexican suit, and he always brought back some information concerning the raiders; and once he came so near being captured by his old enemy, Fletcher, that it was a wonder how he escaped. But long before this happened Gus Robbins had received his discharge as a minor, and gone back to Foxboro', a wiser if not a happier boy; Bristow had found his way into the military prison at Fort Leavenworth; and the cattle-thieves whom Bob Owens had captured at the squatter's cabin had been turned over to the civil authorities. George did all he could to secure Springer's release, but his efforts were unavailing, and with his companions he was sentenced to the penitentiary for a long term of years. Mr. Wentworth had come out all right. With the aid of his friend, Mr. Holmes, he had gathered up all his cattle that had been stampeded by the Mexican raiders, and rebuilt his ranche in a more substantial manner, and he and his boys made it a point to visit the post very frequently to see the men who had rendered them such signal service.

The months wore on, the raids in Colonel Brown's district grew less and less frequent until they ceased altogether, and then the colonel told George that he might go home if he so desired. He did desire it, for he was growing tired of life among the soldiers, and besides, he knew it would be a waste of time for him to remain at the fort when he could no longer be of any use there. So, after taking leave of the officers and of the men who had accompanied him on his expeditions, he mounted his horse, took his pack-mule by the halter and set out. The troopers, who had assembled at the gate to see him go, cheered him lustily as he rode through their ranks, and George carried away with him the assurance that their feelings toward him were very unlike those with which they had regarded him when he first made his appearance at the fort.

Sergeant Owens never lost the position he held in the estimation of both officers and men. He did his duty faithfully, never squandered a cent of his pay at the sutler's store, and at last had the satisfaction of telling himself that he had refunded every cent of the *Mail Carrier's* money, interest included. He kept up a regular correspondence with his father, who told him he was proud of the record he had won, and said everything he could to encourage him. One thing that pleased Bob was the knowledge of the fact that everybody in and about Rochdale was familiar with his history. They knew just what he had done when the steamer Sam Kendall was burned, and the particulars of his exploit on the Staked Plains had been published in the papers. He would go home a hero, instead of sneaking back like a thief in the night; and that is something that runaway boys don't often do.

George Ackerman was glad to get back to his ranche again. He thoroughly enjoyed the quiet life he led there, it was so different from the life of bustle and excitement he had led at the fort. One bright moonlight night, while he was pacing up and down the porch, thinking over old times, and wondering what Bob Owens and the rest of the boys were doing at the fort, he was aroused from the reverie into which he had fallen by the sound of horses' hoofs on the trail. He stopped abruptly, and after listening a moment heard the clanking of sabres mingling with the sound of the horses' feet. Greatly surprised, George descended the steps, and walking out to the trail discovered a long line of horsemen approaching. There was no need that he should ask who they were or where they came from, for as soon as they saw him they greeted him vociferously. They were troopers from Fort Lamoine. They rode on past the ranche, but two men who were riding at the head of the column turned off and came up to him. One was Mr. Gilbert and the other was Captain Clinton.

"Why, captain," exclaimed George, "this is an unexpected pleasure. May I ask where you are going? You'll not march any farther to-night?"

"No, we're not going any farther," was the answer. "I was about to camp near Mr. Gilbert's ranche, but when I happened to mention your name, he told me that you lived only ten miles away; so I came on, thinking that perhaps you would like to see the boys again for the last time. We're going up to Fort Lincoln to join General Terry," continued the captain, as he dismounted and gave his horse up to one of George's herdsmen. "That's in Dakota, you know. A determined—and, I hope, successful—effort is about to be made to crush that old rascal, Sitting Bull, by throwing three strong columns upon him—one under Crook from the south, another under Gibbon from the west, and the third under Terry from the east. There's where your old friends the 'Brindles' are going. I suppose it doesn't make any difference to you where we camp?"

"Of course not," replied George. "There is plenty of grass and water close at hand. Come into the house, both of you. I want to hear all about that great expedition."

Were there not exciting times in the ranche that night? and didn't George find the greatest satisfaction in acting as host to the men with whom he had so often messed at the fort? The supper was the best the house could afford, and all the officers in the column sat down to it. When they had talked themselves out, and were about to go to camp, George asked and obtained permission for Sergeant Owens and all the members of his old squad to come in and visit him. Then there was another supper to be eaten and another long conversation to be had, and the consequence was that when reveille was sounded no one in that ranche had had a wink of sleep.

Bob Owens rode away with his command that morning, and it was a long time before George heard of him again. He left Fort Lincoln with General Terry, went off with Custer on that memorable scout, and when that officer divided his command into three detachments, Sergeant Owens was one of those who were detailed to remain behind with the packs. He heard all of that terrible fight on that bright Sunday afternoon when Reno was defeated and Custer fell with so many of his devoted followers. He took part in the closing scenes of it, for when the packs were ordered up, about six o'clock in the evening, he was under fire from that time until nine, and saw eighteen of his companions killed and forty-six wounded. He marched back to Fort Lincoln with the remnants of the expedition, which had been whipped at every point by the wily old savage it had hoped to crush, and was ordered to Fort Leavenworth, where he received his honorable discharge. Then he went home, and he is there now, living on the best of terms with everybody, especially David Evans. Although he was kept in the army long months beyond his time, he does not complain, for it gives him the opportunity to refer, when speaking of his frontier experience, to the "time when he was with Custer."

George Ackerman is living in his Texas home, managing his own affairs with the assistance of an occasional word from Mr. Gilbert, and keeping up a regular correspondence with his friend Bob Owens, whom he hopes some day to see at his ranche again. He has never heard from his uncle John or from Ned since he parted from them in Galveston. George has seen some stirring times during his life, and has learned how to enjoy himself in a quiet way. He has accumulated a large fund of stories during his travels, and takes pleasure in relating them to any attentive listener. Of all the numerous adventures in which he had borne a part, he delights most to talk about those that befell him during his LIFE AMONG THE SOLDIERS.

* * * * * *

Harry Castlemon

Choose from Thousands of 1stWorldLibrary Classics By

A. M. Barnard
Ada Leverson
Adolphus William Ward
Aesop
Agatha Christie
Alexander Aaronsohn
Alexander Kielland
Alexandre Dumas
Alfred Gatty
Alfred Ollivant
Alice Duer Miller
Alice Turner Curtis
Alice Dunbar
Allen Chapman
Alleyne Ireland
Ambrose Bierce
Amelia E. Barr
Amory H. Bradford
Andrew Lang
Andrew McFarland Davis
Andy Adams
Angela Brazil
Anna Alice Chapin
Anna Sewell
Annie Besant
Annie Hamilton Donnell
Annie Payson Call
Annie Roe Carr
Annonaymous
Anton Chekhov
Archibald Lee Fletcher
Arnold Bennett
Arthur C. Benson
Arthur Conan Doyle
Arthur M. Winfield
Arthur Ransome
Arthur Schnitzler
Arthur Train
Atticus
B.H. Baden-Powell
B. M. Bower
B. C. Chatterjee
Baroness Emmuska Orczy
Baroness Orczy
Basil King
Bayard Taylor
Ben Macomber
Bertha Muzzy Bower
Bjornstjerne Bjornson

Booth Tarkington
Boyd Cable
Bram Stoker
C. Collodi
C. E. Orr
C. M. Ingleby
Carolyn Wells
Catherine Parr Traill
Charles A. Eastman
Charles Amory Beach
Charles Dickens
Charles Dudley Warner
Charles Farrar Browne
Charles Ives
Charles Kingsley
Charles Klein
Charles Hanson Towne
Charles Lathrop Pack
Charles Romyn Dake
Charles Whibley
Charles Willing Beale
Charlotte M. Braeme
Charlotte M. Yonge
Charlotte Perkins Stetson
Clair W. Hayes
Clarence Day Jr.
Clarence E. Mulford
Clemence Housman
Confucius
Coningsby Dawson
Cornelis DeWitt Wilcox
Cyril Burleigh
D. H. Lawrence
Daniel Defoe
David Garnett
Dinah Craik
Don Carlos Janes
Donald Keyhoe
Dorothy Kilner
Dougan Clark
Douglas Fairbanks
E. Nesbit
E. P. Roe
E. Phillips Oppenheim
E. S. Brooks
Earl Barnes
Edgar Rice Burroughs
Edith Van Dyne
Edith Wharton

Edward Everett Hale
Edward J. O'Biren
Edward S. Ellis
Edwin L. Arnold
Eleanor Atkins
Eleanor Hallowell Abbott
Eliot Gregory
Elizabeth Gaskell
Elizabeth McCracken
Elizabeth Von Arnim
Ellem Key
Emerson Hough
Emilie F. Carlen
Emily Bronte
Emily Dickinson
Enid Bagnold
Enilor Macartney Lane
Erasmus W. Jones
Ernie Howard Pie
Ethel May Dell
Ethel Turner
Ethel Watts Mumford
Eugene Sue
Eugenie Foa
Eugene Wood
Eustace Hale Ball
Evelyn Everett-green
Everard Cotes
F. H. Cheley
F. J. Cross
F. Marion Crawford
Fannie E. Newberry
Federick Austin Ogg
Ferdinand Ossendowski
Fergus Hume
Florence A. Kilpatrick
Fremont B. Deering
Francis Bacon
Francis Darwin
Frances Hodgson Burnett
Frances Parkinson Keyes
Frank Gee Patchin
Frank Harris
Frank Jewett Mather
Frank L. Packard
Frank V. Webster
Frederic Stewart Isham
Frederick Trevor Hill
Frederick Winslow Taylor

Friedrich Kerst
Friedrich Nietzsche
Fyodor Dostoyevsky
G.A. Henty
G.K. Chesterton
Gabrielle E. Jackson
Garrett P. Serviss
Gaston Leroux
George A. Warren
George Ade
Geroge Bernard Shaw
George Cary Eggleston
George Durston
George Ebers
George Eliot
George Gissing
George MacDonald
George Meredith
George Orwell
George Sylvester Viereck
George Tucker
George W. Cable
George Wharton James
Gertrude Atherton
Gordon Casserly
Grace E. King
Grace Gallatin
Grace Greenwood
Grant Allen
Guillermo A. Sherwell
Gulielma Zollinger
Gustav Flaubert
H. A. Cody
H. B. Irving
H.C. Bailey
H. G. Wells
H. H. Munro
H. Irving Hancock
H. R. Naylor
H. Rider Haggard
H. W. C. Davis
Haldeman Julius
Hall Caine
Hamilton Wright Mabie
Hans Christian Andersen
Harold Avery
Harold McGrath
Harriet Beecher Stowe
Harry Castlemon
Harry Coghill
Harry Houidini

Hayden Carruth
Helent Hunt Jackson
Helen Nicolay
Hendrik Conscience
Hendy David Thoreau
Henri Barbusse
Henrik Ibsen
Henry Adams
Henry Ford
Henry Frost
Henry James
Henry Jones Ford
Henry Seton Merriman
Henry W Longfellow
Herbert A. Giles
Herbert Carter
Herbert N. Casson
Herman Hesse
Hildegard G. Frey
Homer
Honore De Balzac
Horace B. Day
Horace Walpole
Horatio Alger Jr.
Howard Pyle
Howard R. Garis
Hugh Lofting
Hugh Walpole
Humphry Ward
Ian Maclaren
Inez Haynes Gillmore
Irving Bacheller
Isabel Cecilia Williams
Isabel Hornibrook
Israel Abrahams
Ivan Turgenev
J.G.Austin
J. Henri Fabre
J. M. Barrie
J. M. Walsh
J. Macdonald Oxley
J. R. Miller
J. S. Fletcher
J. S. Knowles
J. Storer Clouston
J. W. Duffield
Jack London
Jacob Abbott
James Allen
James Andrews
James Baldwin

James Branch Cabell
James DeMille
James Joyce
James Lane Allen
James Lane Allen
James Oliver Curwood
James Oppenheim
James Otis
James R. Driscoll
Jane Abbott
Jane Austen
Jane L. Stewart
Janet Aldridge
Jens Peter Jacobsen
Jerome K. Jerome
Jessie Graham Flower
John Buchan
John Burroughs
John Cournos
John F. Kennedy
John Gay
John Glasworthy
John Habberton
John Joy Bell
John Kendrick Bangs
John Milton
John Philip Sousa
John Taintor Foote
Jonas Lauritz Idemil Lie
Jonathan Swift
Joseph A. Altsheler
Joseph Carey
Joseph Conrad
Joseph E. Badger Jr
Joseph Hergesheimer
Joseph Jacobs
Jules Vernes
Julian Hawthrone
Julie A Lippmann
Justin Huntly McCarthy
Kakuzo Okakura
Karle Wilson Baker
Kate Chopin
Kenneth Grahame
Kenneth McGaffey
Kate Langley Bosher
Kate Langley Bosher
Katherine Cecil Thurston
Katherine Stokes
L. A. Abbot
L. T. Meade

L. Frank Baum
Latta Griswold
Laura Dent Crane
Laura Lee Hope
Laurence Housman
Lawrence Beasley
Leo Tolstoy
Leonid Andreyev
Lewis Carroll
Lewis Sperry Chafer
Lilian Bell
Lloyd Osbourne
Louis Hughes
Louis Joseph Vance
Louis Tracy
Louisa May Alcott
Lucy Fitch Perkins
Lucy Maud Montgomery
Luther Benson
Lydia Miller Middleton
Lyndon Orr
M. Corvus
M. H. Adams
Margaret E. Sangster
Margret Howth
Margaret Vandercook
Margaret W. Hungerford
Margret Penrose
Maria Edgeworth
Maria Thompson Daviess
Mariano Azuela
Marion Polk Angellotti
Mark Overton
Mark Twain
Mary Austin
Mary Catherine Crowley
Mary Cole
Mary Hastings Bradley
Mary Roberts Rinehart
Mary Rowlandson
M. Wollstonecraft Shelley
Maud Lindsay
Max Beerbohm
Myra Kelly
Nathaniel Hawthrone
Nicolo Machiavelli
O. F. Walton
Oscar Wilde

Owen Johnson
P.G. Wodehouse
Paul and Mabel Thorne
Paul G. Tomlinson
Paul Severing
Percy Brebner
Percy Keese Fitzhugh
Peter B. Kyne
Plato
Quincy Allen
R. Derby Holmes
R. L. Stevenson
R. S. Ball
Rabindranath Tagore
Rahul Alvares
Ralph Bonehill
Ralph Henry Barbour
Ralph Victor
Ralph Waldo Emmerson
Rene Descartes
Ray Cummings
Rex Beach
Rex E. Beach
Richard Harding Davis
Richard Jefferies
Richard Le Gallienne
Robert Barr
Robert Frost
Robert Gordon Anderson
Robert L. Drake
Robert Lansing
Robert Lynd
Robert Michael Ballantyne
Robert W. Chambers
Rosa Nouchette Carey
Rudyard Kipling
Saint Augustine
Samuel B. Allison
Samuel Hopkins Adams
Sarah Bernhardt
Sarah C. Hallowell
Selma Lagerlof
Sherwood Anderson
Sigmund Freud
Standish O'Grady
Stanley Weyman
Stella Benson
Stella M. Francis

Stephen Crane
Stewart Edward White
Stijn Streuvels
Swami Abhedananda
Swami Parmananda
T. S. Ackland
T. S. Arthur
The Princess Der Ling
Thomas A. Janvier
Thomas A Kempis
Thomas Anderton
Thomas Bailey Aldrich
Thomas Bulfinch
Thomas De Quincey
Thomas Dixon
Thomas H. Huxley
Thomas Hardy
Thomas More
Thornton W. Burgess
U. S. Grant
Upton Sinclair
Valentine Williams
Various Authors
Vaughan Kester
Victor Appleton
Victor G. Durham
Victoria Cross
Virginia Woolf
Wadsworth Camp
Walter Camp
Walter Scott
Washington Irving
Wilbur Lawton
Wilkie Collins
Willa Cather
Willard F. Baker
William Dean Howells
William le Queux
W. Makepeace Thackeray
William W. Walter
William Shakespeare
Winston Churchill
Yei Theodora Ozaki
Yogi Ramacharaka
Young E. Allison
Zane Grey